CONTENTS

An Overview of Islam 1
CHAPTER ONE — *The Development of Islam* 2
   Life Before Muhammad 3
   Muhammad—The Great Prophet 2
   The Middle East 5
CHAPTER TWO — *The Spread of Islam* 6
   The Caliphs (632 - 661) 6
   The Umayyads (661 - 750) 7
   The Beginning of Islam Expansion 7
   The Abbasids (750 - 1258) 8
   The Crusades: A Fight for the Holy Lands 9
   The Mongols 10
   Three Powerful Muslim Monarchies 11
      I.   The Ottoman Empire 11
      II.   The Safavid Dynasty 11
      III.   The Mughal Empire 12
   The Rise of the West: Colonialism and its Aftermath 12
CHAPTER THREE — *Teachings and Practices* 14
   The Quran 14
   The Mosque 15
   The Five Pillars of Islam 17
      Pillar I - The Shahada 17
      Pillar II - Salat 18
      Pillar III - Zakat 18
      Pillar IV - Sawm 18
      Pillar V - Hajj 19
CHAPTER FOUR — *Islamic Law* 20
   Sharia 20
   Muslim Actions 20
   Sin and God's Forgiveness 21
      Good Deeds 21
      Major Sins 21
CHAPTER FIVE — *Women in Islam* 22
   Men and Women Are Equal—Or Are They 22
   Muslim Women and What They Wear 23
CHAPTER SIX — *Islamic Sects* 24
   Sunnis and Shiites 24
   Sufism 25
CHAPTER SEVEN — *Arab Contributions* 26
   Islamic Architecture 26
   Islamic Art 27
   Arabic Literature 30
   Arabic Contributions to Science 32
CHAPTER EIGHT — *Islamic Holy Festivals and Holy Days of Observance* 34
CHAPTER NINE — *A Comparison of Islam with Other World Religions* 35
TEST 39
ANSWER KEY 42
BIBLIOGRAPHY & INTERNET SITES 47

Inside Islam © Milliken Publishing Company

An Overview of Islam

Islam is a religion that developed almost 1400 years ago in Mecca (in present-day Saudi Arabia). Today, Islam is the second largest and fastest growing religion in the world. Approximately 1.5 billion Muslims can be found in countries all around the globe.

Islam is an Arabic word, the root of which (*s-l-m*) primarily means "peace," but in a secondary sense means "surrender." In its broadest sense, the word *Islam* means "the peace that comes when one's life is surrendered to God." Muslims submit to God, called *Allah* in Arabic, and follow Islamic teachings.

Islam is a way of life based on the teachings of the prophet Muhammad who lived from 570—632. Muhammad is believed by Muslims to have received revelations from God. These revelations were assembled in a book called the Quran (also, Koran), which Muslims believe contains the actual word of God. The Quran is the Muslim holy book, containing the guidelines by which followers of Allah are to live, which cannot be changed or added to.

Islam provides guidelines for the moral, spiritual, and political organization of society. Thus, Muslims believe all actions must be guided by God's will.

The fundamental concept of Islam is monotheism—the belief that there is one God, Allah—and Muhammad is his messenger and servant. God requires both moral behavior and devotion from Muslims. Muslims believe that they were created to worship and serve God and humanity.

Muslims have six fundamental beliefs called the articles of faith. The six beliefs are: belief in Allah, belief in angels, belief in the previously revealed books of God, belief in all the prophets, belief in the Day of Judgment, and belief in divine laws.

Words to remember:

Islam
Muslim
prophet
Allah
Quran
Muhammad
articles of faith

Chapter One
The Development of Islam

Life Before Muhammad

Before Islam, people living in the Middle East (see map on page 5) were known as Arabs, as they are today. Their native language was and still is Arabic. All Arabs share a common history and culture.

Arabs before Islam were traders, farmers, nomads, and town-dwellers. They had many religions and worshiped a number of gods.

Muslim history begins with the story of Abraham, a prophet. It is believed that Abraham may have lived between 2100 and 1500 B.C. He is regarded by Muslims (and Jews) as the father of their people. Abraham is also considered to be the first monotheist (believer in one God).

Abraham and his wife's servant, Hagar, had a son named Ishmael. Hagar and Ishmael were sent away when Abraham's wife, Sarah, had a son, Isaac.

Hagar and Ishmael traveled to what came to be called the city of Mecca (the birthplace of Islam). There they found a sacred well. This well provided them with the water they needed to live.

When Ishmael grew to be an adult, Abraham visited him in Mecca. There, next to the sacred well, Abraham and Ishmael (a prophet, like his father) built a temple to God. This temple is called the Kaaba. It is the holiest shrine of the Islamic faith. In the wall of the Kaaba, the two prophets placed the Black Stone. Muslims believe the Black Stone fell from heaven as a sign of the first covenant between God and humankind.

Although the Kaaba was built as a temple to God, many Arabs before Islam filled it with idols that represented a number of gods. These Arabs then made pilgrimages there to worship the idols. It was not until Muhammad conquered

Mecca, in 630, that the Kaaba was cleansed of its idols and returned to its original state of holiness as a temple to the one God of Islam—Allah.

Muhammad – The Great Prophet

Islam began with the prophet Muhammad. Although Muhammad (his name means "the praised one") is not the first Islamic prophet, he is believed by Muslims to be the last. The Quran cites Adam as the first prophet, with thousands falling between Adam and Muhammad, but only 25 listed by name. Some of those listed by name include Abraham, Moses, David, and Jesus.

Muhammad was aware of Hebrew and Christian traditions and believed that God had already revealed himself in part through Moses and Jesus. However, Muhammad believed he was chosen to be God's messenger to deliver the final revelations of God to the people.

Muhammad was born in the Arabian city of Mecca, near the coast of the Red Sea in about 570. According to tradition,

---

Abraham's banishment of Hagar and Ishmael is a pivotal moment in the history of monotheism. Jews and Muslims both claim Abraham as their patriarch. Muslims believe themselves descendants of Abraham through Ishmael, and Jews through Isaac.

Words to remember:

Arabs
Abraham
Hagar
Ishmael
Mecca
Kaaba
Black Stone
idol
Allah
Quran

Inside Islam © Milliken Publishing Company

on the night of his birth, a star filled the sky with a bright light.

Muhammad's parents died when he was young, so he was raised by his uncle. As a young man, Muhammad worked as a trade agent for a wealthy widow. At the age of twenty-five, he

According to Islam, the angel Gabriel spoke to Muhammad.

Words to remember:

**Muhammad
revelations
angel Gabriel
monotheism
idolatry
persecuted
Hegira
Prophet's Tomb**

married this woman (who was fifteen years older than he) and had several children with her.

Muhammad was a successful caravan merchant. In the course of his many journeys, Muhammad had repeated encounters with Jews and Christians. Through them, he became interested in religious questions and grew increasingly uncomfortable with worldliness, greed, and the pagan worship in Mecca. He began to meditate in a cave on the mountain, Hira, outside the city.

There, one night, at age 40, in about 610, Muhammad is said to have received the first of his revelations from God. The angel Gabriel appeared to him and commanded him to recite words that later became part of the Quran. "Recite," Gabriel said, "in the name of the Lord who created man from clots of blood. Your Lord is the Most Bountiful One, who by the pen taught man what he did not know."

Initially frightened, Muhammad came to accept the revelations which were from then on frequently imparted to him. In 613, Muhammad began preaching the message of monotheism—a belief in the one true God. He also taught that idolatry was wrong. This concept was highly controversial, as Arabs had been worshipping a number of gods for many years.

At first, Islam was merely a local religion led by Muhammad, and Meccans tolerated his preaching. Some laughed at Muhammad and thought his teachings odd. But as he grew more confident and uncompromising, condemning the idolatry and immorality of his fellow townsmen, Muhammad was increasingly seen as a danger to the existing way of life and a threat to the Meccan economy. Merchants, in particular, feared that if Arabs became followers of Muhammad and stopped making pilgrimages to Mecca to worship idols at the Kaaba, they would stop spending money there, and the

The Life of Muhammad (570–632)

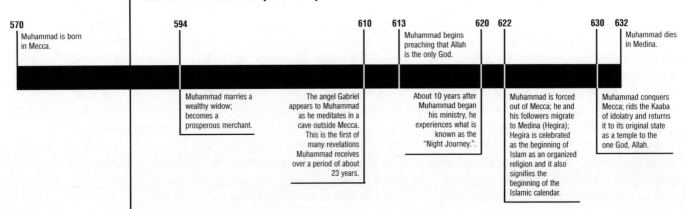

Inside Islam © Milliken Publishing Company

merchants would no longer prosper. So, Muhammad and his followers were persecuted for their beliefs and for their disruption of Meccan life.

Fleeing persecution, Muhammad organized an exodus out of Mecca in 622. He and his small band of followers moved to the nearby city of Medina, 250 miles north, where they were welcomed. This migration is known as the Hegira. This momentous event is important for two reasons: it signifies the beginning of the Islamic calendar; and it recognizes the beginning of Islam as an organized religion.

While Muhammad was in Medina, he attempted to form alliances with Jews and Christians there on the basis of what he believed to be strong common elements in these three monotheistic religions. When his overtures failed, Muhammad began to define Islam differently. He changed the direction of prayer from Jerusalem to Mecca—an act whose political ramifications are still being felt today.

A skilled military leader, Muhammad resisted attacks on Medina by forces from Mecca and successfully led his own attack on Mecca with an army of 10,000 men in 630. Many people who once rejected Islam now embraced it. Muhammad ordered the destruction of idols that surrounded the Kaaba and restored the site to its original state—a temple to the one and only God, Allah.

Today, the Kaaba is Islam's holiest site.

Not long after Muhammad realized his quest for an Arab Islamic state—he ruled almost the entire Arabian peninsula—he died in Medina unexpectedly of fever on June 8, 632. His tomb in Medina is known as the Prophet's Tomb and it, too, is one of Islam's holy sites.

Muhammad was a skilled military leader as well as a prophet.

Section Review

1. How is Islam similar to Christianity and Judaism?
2. How is the role of prophet different in Islam than in other religions?
3. How is Muhammad different from other prophets you are familiar with?
4. How is Islam similar to your religion?
5. Why do you think Islam was feared and rejected at first?

Essay Ideas:

1. Compare Islam's holiest site (Kaaba) to a site you consider holy. Do you feel such sites are important, or perhaps irrelevant? Why?
2. Islam emphasizes moral behavior. What morals, if any, do you feel our society lacks today? If so, what do you feel has contributed to this situation? How do you think these can be reinstated?
3. People often stereotype people of other religions. What could you do to help dispel some of these stereotypes?
4. Name some material objects you feel people in our society worship. Tell why you think these things are worshiped.
5. Write about people today whom you feel are persecuted for their beliefs.
6. Imagine that God sent an angel with a message for you to give to the world. What might that message be?

Inside Islam © Milliken Publishing Company

THE MIDDLE EAST

Islam originated in an area known today as the Middle East. The Middle East is home to a large group of people known as Arabs who speak Arabic as their native language and share a common culture and history. Smaller ethnic groups living in this area include Iranians, Turks, Armenians, Copts, Jews, Greeks, and Kurds.
Most people living in the Middle East are Muslims.

The map above shows the geographic area known as Arabia in the year 610.

1. *Mecca is the birthplace of Islam. Look at this area on the map (left). Now circle the same area in blue on the map below and write its modern-day name.*

2. *The Middle East covers parts of northern Africa, southwestern Asia, and southeastern Europe. Scholars disagree on which countries make up the Middle East. Many say the region is comprised of these 17 countries:* **Bahrain, Cyprus, Egypt, Iran, Iraq, Israel, Jordan, Kuwait, Lebanon, Oman, Qatar, Saudi Arabia, Sudan, Syria, Turkey, United Arab Emirates, and Yemen.** *Label these countries on the map below.*

3. *Pakistan, India, and Afghanistan also have large Muslim populations. Label these countries in green on the map below.*

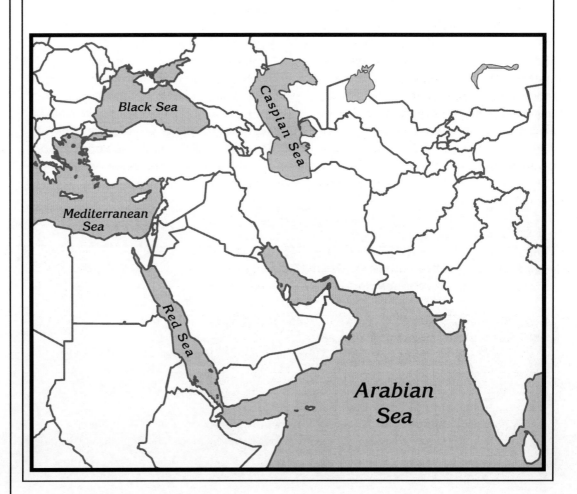

Inside Islam © Milliken Publishing Company

Chapter Two
The Spread of Islam

The Caliphs (632 – 661)

Muhammad's death in 632 created a problem for the Muslim community. Muhammad had no sons and had not appointed a successor. Thus, in keeping with Arab tradition, upon his death, Muhammad's closest disciples met to elect his replacement. His followers disagreed about whom their new leader should be. (Later you will see how this issue divided the Muslim world.)

A *caliph* (from the Arabic word *khalifah* meaning "successor," or "representative") is the secular and religious leader of the Islamic community. Caliphs are elected for life. The first four caliphs (or successors of Muhammad) are known as the Rightly Guided Caliphs. They are called this because each one was believed to have lead an exemplary life and to have worked hard to help Muhammad achieve his goal—spreading Islam to other lands. These caliphs included Abu Bakr, Umar, Uthman, and Ali. They ruled from the city of Medina.

The first caliph, Abu Bakr, was Muhammad's father-in-law—the father of his second wife. He ruled for two years (632-634). Though Abu Bakr did not greatly expand Islam, he was able to subdue revolts led by various Arabian tribes. Muslims were successful in converting these tribes to Islam.

Before Abu Bakr died in 634, he named Umar as his successor. Umar ruled for 10 years (634-644). During this time, the Arabs were intent on conquering neighboring peoples. Umar made it his goal to conquer the Middle East. At the end of his rule, Muslims had conquered Syria, Palestine, Egypt, and most of Iraq. (Refer to the map on page 5 that depicts the Middle East.)

Uthman was appointed caliph after Umar. He ruled from 644 to 656. During Uthman's rule, Muslims completed their conquest of Iran and spread Islam across northern Africa. However, it was also during this time that Muslim political and religious unity ended due to the eruption of political conflicts. Uthman's enemies accused him of caring too much about wealth and material things. Eventually, he was killed.

The last of the Rightly Guided Caliphs was Ali, who ruled from 656 to 661. As Muhammad's son-in-law, he was the closest living relative to Muhammad. He had been asked to be the third caliph, but had refused. When asked a second time, Ali agreed to rule.

By the end of their rule, the Rightly Guided Caliphs had been successful in converting the peoples of many lands to

Words to remember:

Caliph

Rightly Guided Caliphs: Abu Bakr, Umar, Uthman, Ali

Medina

The map below shows the growth of the Islamic state during the reign of the Rightly Guided Caliphs. Compare it to the map of the Middle East today on page 5.

Inside Islam © Milliken Publishing Company

Islam. They also helped create a vast new Islamic empire that was controlled by Arabian Muslims.

Section Review:

1. How were the Rightly Guided Caliphs successful?
2. What does the word *caliph* mean?

The Umayyads (661 – 750)

After the four Rightly Guided Caliphs, the Umayyad dynasty of caliphs ruled the Islamic empire. From this time on, the position of caliph was an inherited one. The Umayyads did not rule from Medina like their predecessors. They made Damascus their capital.

THE BEGINNING OF ISLAM EXPANSION

The map below depicts the areas to which Islam spread from the time of Muhammad's death to the fall of the Umayyad caliphs. After reading the information below, create a map key to identify the land acquisitions of each ruling group. Be sure to include dates in your map key.

1. *At the time of Muhammad's death (632), Islam was practiced by Muslims living in Arabia.*

2. *By the end of their rule, the Rightly Guided Caliphs (632-661) had succeeded in spreading Islam across North Africa, Egypt, Syria, Palestine, Iran, and Iraq.*

3. *The Umayyads (661-750) continued conquering lands and converting people to Islam. Their empire included North Africa and Spain (west) and Afghanistan and central Asia (east).*

4. *Label the country that defeated the Muslims at the Battle of Tours, plus all bodies of water.*

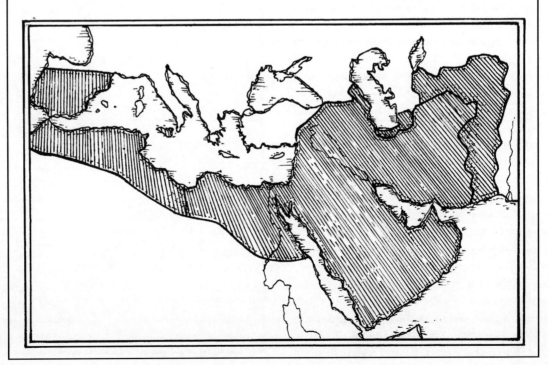

Inside Islam © Milliken Publishing Company

Under the Umayyads, the Islamic state developed into an imperial power. The Muslims expanded their empire to include Afghanistan and central Asia in the east and across northern Africa and into Spain in the west. This expansion of Islam greatly increased the number of non-Arab Muslims. (An attempt was also made to conquer France at the Battle of Tours. However, the French, under Charles Martel, defeated the Muslims. Many historians view this battle as one of the most important ever fought because it resulted in Christianity, not Islam, becoming the dominant religion in Europe.)

The Umayyad caliphs lived more like kings than religious leaders. They reorganized the government and created postal routes. They built magnificent mosques. And though these changes were beneficial for many Muslims, they also ultimately led to the destruction of the Umayyads.

The vast Umayyad empire was besieged by many social and economic problems. Some of these problems stemmed from the newly conquered peoples. For the first time, many new Islamic lands contained more non-Arab Muslims than Arab Muslims. These new Muslims were not chosen for important government jobs, had to pay higher taxes, and earned less money for serving in the army than Arab Muslims. This made the non-Arab Muslims angry and led to many revolts against the Umayyads.

Further complicating matters, the Muslim religion suffered internal theological and political disputes that resulted in a splintering of the religion into two groups—the Shiites, who believed only descendants of Ali (the last of the Rightly Guided Caliphs and a descendant of Muhammad) should hold the title of caliph, and the Sunnis who believed that any sufficiently pious and qualified person could be caliph. Dissension was apparent in many areas of the Arab Empire.

Eventually, a group of Muslims called the Abbasids began to strongly support the new Muslims. The Abbasids believed the new Muslims should have the same rights as the Arabs, regardless of their ethnic background. In 750, they overthrew the Umayyads. Thus began the rule of the Abbasids. Their rule lasted until 1258.

Section Review:

1. What two branches of Islam formed during Umayyad rule and why?
2. What caused the fall of the Umayyad dynasty?

The Abbasids (750 – 1258)

The Abbasids ruled the Arab Empire from 750 to 1258. Their first 100 years is called the Golden Age of Islam. It was during this period that many positive changes occurred in the empire. After this time, many problems arose among the Muslims and their leaders.

Unlike the Umayyads, the Abbasids did not strive to greatly expand their empire. It had already grown so large, that they had to work hard to keep it united. As it was, an Arab no longer meant "a person from Arabia." At this point, an Arab signified someone who spoke Arabic. Basically, the only Arab influence left in the Arab Empire was the Islamic religion and the Arabic language. The many new cultures and customs that had been acquired during expansion had created a whole new kind of Arab.

So instead of focusing on greater expansion of the empire, the Abbasids focused on turning Baghdad, Iraq, into a major world trading center. To accomplish this goal, the Abbasids first moved the capital of the Arab empire from Damascus to Baghdad in 762. Here, the centralized monarchy of the Abbasids operated from a huge complex called the City of Peace. This complex included a great mosque, the caliph's incredible palace, and the magnificent homes of public officials.

Words to remember:

**Umayyads
imperial power
Abbasids
Battle of Tours**

**non-Arab Muslims/
new Muslims**

**Sunnis
Shiites**

Inside Islam © Milliken Publishing Company

To further aid in the creation of a great trading center, the Abbasids took advantage of the Persian Gulf and the Euphrates River for transporting goods. Products came from east Africa, Arabia, India, southeast Asia, and China by way of the Persian Gulf. Goods from northern Africa, Egypt, and the Mediterranean flowed along the Euphrates River. Baghdad became the center of an enormous trade empire.

Due to the increased number of countries trading in Baghdad, Islamic arts and sciences also flourished during the rule of the Abbasids. Works of such great Greek philosophers as Plato and Aristotle were translated into Arabic; several schools of Islamic law were created; a research library called the House of Wisdom was established; and the Quran and Arabic grammar were big topics of study.

With access to many different parts of the world, life changed rapidly and dramatically in the Arab empire. Trade made many Arabs wealthy. Even farmers prospered, thanks to advances in farming methods. And new customs evolved. For example, rather than wearing the customary Arab robe, men began wearing pants.

Also new under Abbasid rule was the emergence of Sufism. (Sufis are Islamic mystics who take vows of poverty and perform acts of physical deprivation such as fasting and going without sleep in order to achieve a more perfect unity with God. See Chapter 6 for a more lengthy discussion.) Sufis can be Sunnis or Shiites.

With all of the changes that took place in the Arab empire under the Abbasids, it is no surprise that ruling the Arab empire was becoming too much for one caliph. The empire was so large that it began breaking up into smaller, independent kingdoms. From 929 to 1031, three caliphs were ruling in the empire. There were the Abbasids in Iraq, the Umayyads in Spain, and another caliph dynasty in northern Africa. In fact, from the mid-900s until the fall of the Abbasids, many caliphs were considered weak leaders, often forced to follow the commands of powerful military dictators.

Also during this time of weakness, groups of Muslim Turks from central Asia began invading the Arab empire. The most noteworthy were the Seljuk Turks. This group of non-Arab invaders conquered Baghdad in 1055 and then went on to conquer Syria and Palestine. By the end of the 1000s, the Abbasid empire began to deteriorate. Independent dynasties began to appear. In 1258, what was left of the Abbasid government was destroyed by the Mongols from China when they conquered Baghdad.

By the end of Abbasid rule, the culture of the Islamic empire was vast, rich, and diverse. While this very richness and diversity inevitably lead to the decentralization of political power and contributed greatly to the fall of the Abassids, this cultural diversity exists today and is among the great Abassid legacies.

Section Review:

1. Do you think it was wise of the Abbasids to stop trying to expand their empire? Why?
2. Why did Islamic arts and sciences flourish when Baghdad became a major world trade center?
3. How did life change for many Arabs after Baghdad became a center for world trade?

*The Crusades:
A Fight for the Holy Land*

Subsequent to the Battle of Tours in A.D. 732 in which the Christian French defeated the invading Muslim armies of the Ummayad empire (a defeat which halted the spread of Islam in Europe), contact between Christians and Muslims had mainly been commercial and intellectual—a fruitful exchange of goods and ideas. Exposure to Europeans through trade had left Muslims with the

Words to remember:

**Abbasids
Golden Age of Islam

Arab (at time of Abbasid Empire)

Damascus
Baghdad
City of Peace
Persian Gulf
Euphrates River
Sufism
mystics
Seljuk Turks
Mongols**

impression that, compared to themselves, Christians were crude, ignorant, and barbaric. Conversely, Europeans became aware of the extent of Muslim wealth, luxury, sophistication, and learnedness.

Given this disparity, and the obvious supremacy of Islamic culture at the time, Muslims were shocked when bands of common European peoples, poorly equipped and poorly trained, set out to capture the Holy Land in 1096, launching a series of bloody battles or *crusades* that took place over a period of two hundred years. (The word *crusade* comes from the Latin word *crux*, meaning "cross." Members of the crusading Christian armies sewed the symbol of the cross of Christ on their tunics.)

There were seven crusades altogether, during which the warring parties won and lost and won and lost the coveted city of Jerusalem and bits and pieces of surrounding land. The first crusade (1096–1099) resulted in the European crusaders arriving in Jerusalem and capturing the city after six weeks of fighting. Less than fifty years later, the second crusade (1147-1149) lead to the Muslim Turks winning the city back. The third crusade (1182-1192), the fourth (1201-1204), and subsequent lesser crusades marked additional failed attempts on the part of German, French and British crusaders to take back the Holy Land. Overall, the Crusades were a military disaster for the Europeans. And while they were devastating for Muslims in the vicinity of Jerusalem, for the majority of Muslims in Iraq, Iran, Afghanistan, Central Asia, and India, they were distant and minor border conflicts.

The effects of two centuries of Western attempts to diminish the Muslim stronghold in the Holy Land perhaps effected the West more deeply than it did the East. While the West suffered military humiliation and defeat, Western exposure to the superiority and richness of Islamic culture elevated the West immeasurably. From the Muslims, Europeans learned shipbuilding, mapmaking, and better ways of making war. They acquired new tastes in food and clothing and an appetite for travel. Ironically, the Crusades hastened the rise of the West and shocked Muslims with the realization that their supremacy would not go untested.

The Mongols

The invasion of the Mongols in the 13th century marked a turning point in Islamic history. Having grown (over a period of 600 years) from a tiny religious community at Medina in Arabia to a vast Islamic empire with holdings in Africa, Asia, Europe, and the Middle East, the fall of Baghdad in 1258 to savage tribal warriors from the north began an era of unprecedented foreign rule. It was the first time since the reign of the Rightly Guided Caliphs 600 years earlier that a significant part of the Islamic world was dominated by a non-Muslim power.

These ruthless Mongol invaders, once a loose band of nomadic tribes inhabiting the inhospitable northern lands of Mongolia, Manchuria, and Siberia, unified in the 1100s under the leadership of Genghis Khan. The Mongols became one of the most vicious and disciplined fighting forces in history.

In 1258, the Mongols (by then rulers of the world's largest land empire) executed the last Abassid caliph and captured Baghdad—the capital city of the Islamic empire—completely destroying it.

While the Mongol invasion marked a suspension of Islamic political and military power, the same cannot be said of Islamic religion and culture. The Mongols, themselves, became Islamic converts and the Mongolian empire became a vehicle for the spread of Islamic culture and religion around the world.

During the rule of the Mongols, Islam spread to western Africa, present-day Malaysia, Indonesia, China, and Africa south of the Sahara. Due to an increase in trade, people of many different

Words to remember:

**Mongols
Genghis Khan
conversions**

cultures came into contact with one another serving to increase the exchange of ideas. One of these "ideas" was Islam which proved to be well received, and many large-scale conversions to Islam took place. These conversions, in turn, led to a very socially and culturally diverse Muslim population whose global power intensified in the years to come.

Section Review:

1. Why did the Muslim world become so diverse during the Mongol Empire?
2. Why did the conversion of large numbers of people to Islam occur during Mongol rule?

After the Mongols: Three Powerful Muslim Monarchies

In the post-Mongol period, there were three main centers of power in the Islamic world: the Ottoman Empire (originating in Turkey), the Safavid dynasty of Iran (the Safavids gave Iran the geographical shape which it has today), and the Mughal Empire of India.

I. The Ottoman Empire

The Ottoman Empire existed from about 1300 to 1922. It was the world's most powerful empire in the 1500s and 1600s. The Ottomans were nomadic Turkish tribes that emigrated from central Asia to the Middle East. They declared themselves experts and devout followers of Sunni Islam (a group encompassing 90% of all Muslims today).

In 1453, the Ottomans conquered Constantinople (now Istanbul), the capital of the once very powerful Byzantine Empire. This led to the collapse of an empire that had controlled parts of Asia Minor and southeastern Europe for almost 1000 years. Constantinople became the new capital of the Ottoman Empire and also the center of Islamic thought.

By the mid 1500s, the Ottoman Empire included Asia Minor (now Turkey), the Balkans, and parts of north Africa and present-day Iran, Saudi Arabia, and Syria. Though many of these lands were already Arab lands filled with Muslims, the Ottomans continued to spread the Islamic faith to lands in which Islam did not exist.

One particular Ottoman ruler, Sultan Suleiman I, also known as Suleiman the Magnificent, because of the impact he had on cultural achievements during his reign (1520–1566). Islamic arts and sciences flourished, and the Muslim world experienced its most profound level of unity since the time of Abbasid rule.

Even though the Ottomans were Muslims, people under their rule were permitted to practice any faith they chose. The two largest non-Muslim groups were Christians and Jews.

In the 1700s and 1800s, the Ottoman Empire began to decline. Its deterioration of size and power was due in large part to the development of new, strong European countries. By the early 1900s, European colonial powers dominated a large part of the Muslim world and had a big impact on it—economically, politically, and culturally. This once powerful empire dissolved completely with the creation of the nation of Turkey in 1923 in the aftermath of the Ottoman defeat in World War I.

II. The Safavid Dynasty

The Safavid dynasty in Iran was the main rival of the Ottomans. This group originated as Sufis in northwestern Iran but converted to Shiism along with the rest of Iran in the 1500s. (Iran had previously been a Sunni state.) The Safavids became very powerful leaders of the Shiite Turks.

The Safavids and the Ottomans fought against each other during the mid-1600s. Neither side won. The most significant outcome was a devastating loss of resources for both sides.

The Safavids continued to rule Iran until 1722 when the empire began to crumble.

Words to remember:

Ottoman Empire

nomadic Turkish tribes

emigrated
Sunni Islam
Byzantine Empire
Sultan Suleiman I

III. The Mughal Empire

The Mughal Empire of India was founded in 1526 by Prince Babur from central Asia. Although Babur's army was small, it was still able to defeat larger Indian armies with the help of firearms. This empire peaked during the reign of Akbar (1555-1605). During his reign, Akbar's empire encompassed two-thirds of south Asia, including Bangladesh, north and central India, Pakistan, and most of present-day Afghanistan. Even though it was officially a Sunni empire, many high offices were held by Shiites. The empire began its decline in the 1700s and ended in 1858.

Section Review:

1. Identify one significant way in which the Safavids differed from the Ottomans?
2. How can it be said that both the Safavids and the Ottomans "lost" the wars they fought against each other?
3. What made Prince Babur's army so powerful?
4. What flexibility did the Mughals openly allow regarding religion that the Ottomans and Safavids did not?

The Rise of the West: Colonialism and Its Aftermath

The rhythms of history are mysterious. Civilizations flourish and then vanish leaving only traces of what once was a dwelling, a village, a city, an empire. The sudden emergence and rapid spread of Islamic civilization in the 7th century took place against the backdrop of the waning Byzantine Empire (what remained of the once great Roman Empire) and the dying out of the empire of Persia. Nearly a hundred years of fighting between these two great cultures (both of whom controlled vast swaths of land) weakened them, leaving room for the rise of a new and perhaps unexpected power—a tiny religious cult from Mecca, Arabia, under the charismatic leadership of the prophet Muhammad. Muhammad was astonishingly effective in unifying the many diverse tribes inhabiting Arabia. Under his great leadership as both a spiritual and military leader, Islam spread at a breathless pace all over the world, enjoying an uncontested reign for six centuries, until various powers from the north began to slowly pick away at its supremacy. As previously mentioned, the Crusades (the numerous attempts of Western Europeans to capture and control the city of Jerusalem) were mildly disruptive to the cohesion of the Islamic empire, but failed to threaten its world dominion. The bigger blow came in the 13th century from another northern tribe—the Mongols—whose ruthless fighting tactics crushed much of Islamic civilization and considerably lessened its strength in the world.

Throughout the 15th and 16th centuries, Islamic culture continued under the rule of the Ottoman, the Safavid (Persian), and the Mughal (Indian) empires, but never again attained the unified strength it once had.

For just as mysterious as the rise of Muhammad in the early 7th century was the emergence of the once backward

Words to remember:

Safavid dynasty
Iran
Sufis
Shiism
Mughal Empire
Prince Babur
Akbar

In 1798, Napoleon stormed Alexandria, defeated the Muslims at the foot of the Great Pyramids, and occupied Cairo. While his occupation was brief, his arrival in Egypt symbolized the decline of Muslim civilization.

culture of Western Europeans north of the Alps who had been languishing (in the Middle Ages of European history) in a primitive agrarian society. As discussed earlier, when Muslims encountered these people during the Crusades, they regarded them as barbaric, uneducated, and unsophisticated. A combination of things—foremost, the scientific advances in the West during the 17th and 18th centuries, and the industrial revolution of the 18th and 19th centuries—led to their growing strength.

By the late 18th century, the once impervious civilization of Islam began to suffer the intrusion of the West. In 1798, Napoleon horrified Muslims everywhere by conquering Egypt. While the British defeated him three days later, Napoleon's arrival on Muslim soil was symbolic of the waning cultural and political power of the Arab empire and growing European might.

The last half of the 1800s and the early 1900s saw an expanded European presence in the Muslim world. During this time, Europe either directly or indirectly controlled all Muslim countries with the exception of Arabia, Iran, and Turkey. These countries were divided into more than 15 European colonies and protectorates. (A protectorate is an area that is only partially controlled by a colonial power.)

The last act of European colonialism was the division of the Arab territories of the Ottoman Empire after World War I. Colonialism ended after World War II when England and France withdrew from most of their colonies. The gradual emergence of independent Muslim states after 1947 occurred in some cases though peaceful negotiation, and in others, through bloody wars for independence (as happened in Algeria).

By the mid-1970s, most Muslim territories had established independence, but it was a freedom colored (even soured) by the humiliating legacy of colonialism. Once a vast and imposing empire, the Muslim world is now a collection of nation-states haunted by the grandeur of its past. Struggling to understand their newly-defined relationship with the West, many Muslims are still animated by a quest for the political unity they once enjoyed and are understandably undergoing a difficult crisis of identity.

Section Review:

1. Why was the Muslim world horrified when Napoleon conquered Egypt?
2. What do you think contributed to the decline of Islamic civilization and the rise of the West?
3. If you were a Muslim today, you might have mixed or complicated feelings toward the West. Explain.

Words to remember:

**Napoleon
colonies
protectorate
colonialism**

Essay Ideas:

1. Do you believe the position of a high official should be inherited or elected?
2. Compare the inequalities that existed between "new" Muslims and "old" Muslims to the inequalities that exist among various groups today.
3. How different do you think Europe might be today if the French had lost the Battle of Tours?
4. Think about the office of President of the United States and the reign of a king or queen. Which title would you rather hold and why?
5. Imagine you are living under the rule of one of the dynasties featured in this chapter. Describe the events of one day in your life.

Chapter Three
Teaching and Practices

The Quran

The Quran is the holy book of Muslims. It is one of the greatest and most widely read books in the world. Its teachings are the heart of Islamic belief, and its basic message is that there is no god but Allah, and Muhammad is his prophet.

Muslims believe the Quran contains the actual words of God. These words came in the form of revelations. These revelations are believed to have been sent from God through the angel Gabriel to the prophet, Muhammad. Muhammad then passed them on to his followers who became known as Muslims.

Muhammad was born in Mecca in 570. Muslims believe he received his first revelation in 610 when he was about 40 years old. It is believed that the angel Gabriel told Muhammad to "recite."

For the next 22 years or so, until his death in 632, Muhammad continued receiving revelations from God. After he died, Muhammad's followers compiled the revelations into sacred book. According to Muslim teachings, Muhammad either dictated the words to scribes, or they wrote down or memorized the revelations. The final form of the Quran was determined by the third caliph (the third successor to Muhammad), Uthman.

The Quran is considered perfect and is written in Arabic. It cannot be added to or changed. This protects it from any type of corruption. Though the Quran has been translated, Muslims believe translations are uninspired and not the true word of God. Therefore, Muslims have always studied the Quran in its original form. Even young children must recite the words in Arabic, regardless of whether they fully understand them or not. Students are encouraged to memorize as much of the Quran as they can. This requires great devotion and diligence as the Quran contains 114 surahs (chapters). The surahs range in length from a few lines to several hundred verses. In its entirety, the Quran is a little shorter than the New Testament.

Copies of the Quran are often beautifully printed and decorated. They are treated very carefully and are touched only after a person has ritually cleansed himself or herself. To show how highly regarded the Quran is, it is often stored in a special box and kept in a special place in the home or mosque.

Considered to be the actual word of God, Muslims use the Quran to guide their every action and thought. It teaches about many things—God, prophets, values, morals, virtues, life, and death.

The central teaching of the Quran is that there is only one God (Allah). God created all things and demands that people submit to him. (Islam means "submission.") Muslims believe that God sent the Quran to serve as a guide for all people to follow as they live their lives.

To show how highly the Quran is regarded, it is often stored in a special box or covering and kept in a special place.

Words to remember:

Quran
angel Gabriel
Muhammad
scribes
caliph
Uthman
surahs
mosque

Inside Islam © Milliken Publishing Company

The Quran teaches about God by giving him such descriptive names as Protector, Great, Merciful, and Guide. It lists 99 names which Muslims can recite and meditate on with the help of a 33-bead rosary.

The Quran also contains teachings concerning prophets. Islamic prophets do not foretell the future. Instead, God sent prophets as messengers to encourage people to worship only him and to teach them how to live according to his laws. The Quran states the existence of thousands of prophets, but only 25 are listed by name. Some of those named include Adam, Abraham, Moses, David, Jesus, and, of course, Muhammad. Adam is believed to be the first prophet, and Muhammad is the last.

Values, morals, and virtues are also covered in the Quran. The holy book teaches that Muslims may not lie, steal, or murder. It does not tolerate mistrust, impatience, or cruelty. The Quran says that Muslims must treat all of God's creation with kindness and compassion.

Muslims are encouraged to be kind, honest, merciful, courageous, compassionate, patient, and polite.

Another principle teaching of the Quran concerns Judgment Day. On this day, the Quran says that all people must stand before God and be accountable for the way they lived their lives. The Quran teaches that life is a test, and we will either be rewarded or punished for our actions after we die. It promises that all who live according to God's word will go to paradise. Muslims believe that those who choose not to follow God's word end up in a fiery hell.

Many specific teachings regarding the daily lives of Muslims are included in the Quran, as well. Muslims must pray daily and show brotherly love to all Muslims, especially their parents and elderly people.

The Quran also includes a variety of other instructions and teachings. For example, it teaches how to organize society and how to implement the law. It contains rules for the structure of family life and rules for good behavior. Every Muslim thought and action must be guided by God's will.

In addition to the Quran, Muslims also consult the sunna to help them lead godly lives. The sunna consists of the actions and words Muhammad did and said during his life. His conduct and words are valuable to Muslims because, along with the Quran, they can help guide Muslims to lead the kind of virtuous life Muhammad did—the kind of godly life God wants them to lead.

Section Review:

1. What is the Quran?
2. Why do Muslims study the Quran in Arabic?
3. What are some of the teachings of the Quran?
4. What virtues and values are Muslims supposed to aspire to?
5. What is the sunna?

The Mosque

The mosque plays an important role in the life of a Muslim. It is a place where Muslims gather to worship God (Allah). Occasionally, mosques may be used for religious education, for social work, as tombs, or as temporary homes

Words to remember:

Allah
Islam
prophets
Adam
Muhammad
Judgment Day
sunna

Muslims sometimes use a 33-bead rosary during prayer.

for traveling scholars.

Mosques can vary in style, depending on the country in which they are located. Some mosques are simply plain assembly halls where Muslims gather to pray. Others, called Cathedral, or Friday mosques, are grand, intricate structures that have been built to accommodate all of the adult Muslims in a community. Regardless of style, all mosques have certain features in common.

Most mosques have a courtyard that is surrounded by four halls. These halls are called iwams. Usually, a fountain is located in the courtyard where Muslims ritually cleanse themselves before prayer.

One of the most distinguishable features of the mosque is the minaret. When Muslims gaze up at this tall, slender tower, they are symbolically looking up to heaven where God is the ultimate ruler. It is from a balcony on this tower that the muezzin (crier) calls Muslims to prayer. (Today, this is usually done electronically, with the help of a loudspeaker system.) In Arabic, the muezzin calls out, "God is great!" He ends with, "There is no god but Allah!"

The walls of the mosque usually feature elaborate decorations. These decorations are always abstract and geometrical, representing divine harmony. Since Muslims are careful to avoid worshipping other gods, there are no distracting pictures of people or animals in mosques. This helps Muslims focus on worshipping only God.

The large inner area of the mosque is usually adorned only with carpets and rugs, and two other objects called the mihrab, and the minbar. The carpets and rugs are used as prayer mats. This area is considered holy ground. Worshippers kneel and bow down with their faces to the ground on these mats when in prayer.

The mihrab is a niche in the wall. It denotes the direction of Mecca, the birthplace of Muhammad. When Muslims pray, they always face Mecca. The minbar is a pulpit. From the minbar, the imam (religious leader) delivers a khutba (sermon) to the people. These sermons are given on Fridays. Fridays are important days of Muslim worship. Every Friday at midday, Muslims gather together at a mosque to honor and worship God.

Mosques are sacred places to Muslims, just as churches and temples are to people of other religions. They must be respected by all who visit, regardless of a person's religious background.

Section Review:

1. What are mosques used for?
2. What are some common features of mosques?

The muezzin (crier) once called Muslims to prayer from the balcony of the minaret by calling out, "God is great!" Today this is usually done electronically.

Inside Islam © Milliken Publishing Company

ISLAMIC MOSQUES

Label the illustrations below depicting the various features of a typical mosque: **Minaret and balcony**, **Mihrab** (niche), **Minbar** (pulpit), **Fountain in courtyard**, **Prayer mats** (holy ground).

Words to remember:

Cathedral/
Friday mosques

courtyard
iwams
minaret
muezzin
mihrab
minbar
imam
khutba

The Five Pillars of Islam

The Quran lists five formal acts of worship all Muslims must fulfill in obedience to God. These acts are called the Pillars of Islam. They are so named because they are likened to the pillars in a mosque that support the building. Like pillars of a building, the Pillars of Islam support Islam's teachings and practices. Anyone who does not fulfill these obligations may be punished by God or by the Islamic state.

The Five Pillars of Islam are as follows: 1. the shahada (declaration of faith); 2. salat (daily worship); 3. zakat (charitable giving); 4. sawm (fasting); and 5. hajj (pilgrimage to Mecca).

Pillar I – *The Shahada*

Shahada is a declaration of faith and means "act of bearing witness." It is the pillar on which the other four pillars are based. This declaration has two parts: 1. The belief that there is no god but Allah; and 2. Muhammad is the Messenger of God. The English translation of the shahada reads, *"I bear witness that there is none worthy of worship except Allah, the One, without any partner. And I bear witness that Muhammad is His servant and His Messenger."* By reciting this statement, Muslims are declaring their belief in one God and that Muhammad is God's messenger. These words of faith are whispered into a baby's ear following birth, and it is the last thing Muslims hope to say at the moment of death.

Pillar II – *Salat*

Salat is prayer. Daily prayer by Muslims is the most important way they can show their devotion to God. Muslims must pray five times a day—at dawn, at midday, in the afternoon, just after sunset, and at night. This practice began after Muhammad's "Night Journey." This miraculous experience involved Muhammad journeying up to the sky with angels. It is believed that he was taken from Mecca to Jerusalem, where he prayed with such earlier prophets as Abraham and Jesus. After praying, Muhammad ascended to heaven where God told him to implement the recitation of prayers five times a day.

The times to pray are determined by the position of the sun. The prayers can be said anywhere, except on Fridays. On Fridays at noon, many Muslims go to worship at a mosque where they are led by an imam (prayer leader). This service lasts from 30 to 60 minutes.

A muezzin (crier) calls Muslims to prayer from the minaret (tower) on the mosque. Before praying, Muslims remove their shoes and ritually wash their hands, face, feet, and parts of their arms and head. This cleansing ritual is symbolic of spiritual purification.

When praying, Muslims always face the direction of Mecca (the birthplace of Muhammad). They also complete a fixed number and sequence of movements during prayer. These movements include prostration, which involves kneeling, bowing, and putting their faces very low to the ground. Men worship separately from the women and children so that they do not distract each other. The actual prayers include the repetition of the phrase "God is greatest," five times, and recitation of verses from the Quran.

Muslims take very seriously the role of prayer in their lives. It is what they consider to be of utmost importance in showing their submission and devotion to God.

Pillar III – *Zakat*

Zakat means "to purify oneself." This duty requires Muslims to "purify" their wealth once a year by sharing a certain percentage (usually about 2.5 percent) of their assets with the needy. It reminds them that all things come from and ultimately belong to God. Zakat is paid like a tax, and the money given benefits mainly welfare organizations, mosques, and Islamic centers.

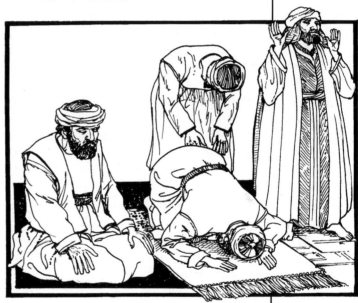

Pillar IV – *Sawm*

Sawm is fasting. It applies to Muslims during the holy month of Ramadan. During Ramadan, Muslims are forbidden to eat and drink during daylight hours. They may eat and drink at night. Fasting is done to help Muslims reflect spiritually, recognize the needs of others, and obey God. Muslims too sick or elderly to observe sawm are expected to provide food to the poor or fast at a later time.

Pillar V – *Hajj*

The fifth Pillar of Islam is called hajj.

Muslim prayer has four stages requiring four different postures, the last two of which—bowing and prostration—express total submission to God.

Hajj is a pilgrimage to Mecca that takes place two months after Ramadan. Every Muslim who is physically able, who is of sound mind, and who can afford the journey is required to make this pilgrimage at least once in his or her lifetime. Muslims from all over the world gather together for this three-day-long experience that involves ceremonies and sacrifice.

Muslims perform hajj for several reasons. One is to visit the holy sites where Islam originated. Another is to see the Kaaba, which Muslims believe is the first place of worship to be built on earth. Hajj is also performed to celebrate God's unity. The gathering of Muslims from all over the world in one spot is symbolic of this unity.

During hajj, men are required to wear two pieces of unsewn white cloth called ihram. Ihram means "garment of consecration." Women are required to wear a long white gown and head scarf.

The ceremonies and sacrifices performed during hajj center around the prophet Abraham, the servant Hagar, and their son, Ishmael. Muslims believe Abraham and Ishmael built the Kaaba— the first temple to God. In one corner of this empty, cube-shaped building, is the Black Stone that Abraham and Ishmael are believed to have put there. (Muslims believe the Black Stone fell from heaven as a sign of the first covenant between God and humankind.)

Over the course of the 3-day event, pilgrims perform such symbolic acts as:

1. Running along a corridor and then taking water from a well (symbolizing Hagar's search for water for her baby son, Ishmael);
2. Standing on a plain outside Mecca, in Arafat (symbolizing the final pilgrimage of Muhammad and the place where Muhammad delivered his farewell sermon);
3. Throwing stones at three pillars (symbolizing Ishmael driving away the temptations of Satan);
4. Sacrificing an animal (symbolizing Abraham's vow to sacrifice his own son Isaac, also a prophet).

Other acts involved in hajj include walking counterclockwise around the Kaaba seven times and trying to kiss the Black Stone.

Once a Muslim has fulfilled the obligation of hajj, al-Hajj can be added at the end of this pilgrim's name.

Section Review:

1. What are the five Pillars of Islam?
2. What are the two parts of the shahada?
3. Why do Muslims face Mecca when they pray?
4. Why do Muslims perform hajj?
5. Tell why you think Muslims consider only the original form of the Quran to be authentic.
6. Explain why you think the Quran is treated with great care.
7. How is the Quran a guide for Muslims?

Words to remember:

shahada
salat
Night Journey
muezzin
zakat
sawm
fasting
Hajj
Mecca
Kaaba
ihram
Abraham
Hagar
Ishmael
Black Stone
Isaac
al-Hajj

Essay Ideas:

1. Compare the Quran to a holy book with which you are familiar.
2. Write how you live your life in ways that are in agreement with the ways the Quran teaches Muslims to live.
3. Compare a mosque and the rituals and activities that occur there to the place where you worship.
4. Write five "pillars" you believe all people should live by.
5. Imagine that you are a Muslim for a day during Ramadan. Write about your day.
6. Write whether you think fulfilling the Five Pillars of Islam would be easy or difficult.

CHAPTER FOUR

Islamic Law

Sharia is the Islamic system of law. It is interpreted with the help of the Quran and the sunna. Though Sharia deals with all aspects of society, Muslims have also been given a set of guidelines to follow concerning their actions.

Islamic Law is a combination of personal morality and civil and criminal law. This type of oneness is in agreement with the Islamic view that there is no difference between the secular and spiritual realms. However, not all actions are treated in the same manner. For example, criminal actions are prosecuted in court, but most other negative actions are considered to be sins and are subject to God's punishment.

Sharia

Sharia is the divinely revealed and inspired Islamic system of law. Sharia is an Arabic word that describes a path leading camels to a watering hole. It implies that if people follow this path, it will lead to Allah.

The main sources of Islamic law are the Quran (the word of God) and the sunna (the collections of stories and sayings that recount the exemplary actions of Muhammad's life). It is these two sources that Muslim scholars use to help them understand and interpret the principles of the Sharia. And though all Islamic law is considered sacred, most sources of Islamic law originate in the sunna, not the Quran.

Since the Quran does not address many specific issues facing society today, Muslim scholars continually find themselves interpreting the law. Their discoveries often become the basis for new laws. Muftis are experts who are able to rule on points of law. Shiites also accept rulings from ayatollahs, their highest religious leaders.

Although most Muslims agree on the fundamental principles of Islam, it is not surprising that scholars often disagree on various interpretations of the law. These differences often lead to different opinions concerning many issues facing society today.

Muslim Actions

In Islamic law, a person's actions can be divided into five categories:

1. those God has commanded (example—Five Pillars);
2. those God has forbidden (examples—stealing, cheating, killing);
3. those God has suggested but not demanded;
4. those God has disapproved of but not specifically forbidden; and
5. those God has kept silent about.

Muslims who do not do what God has commanded, such as performing specific religious duties dictated by the Five Pillars, may be punished by God or the Islamic state. The same is true for the actions God has specifically forbidden. Most of these acts are mentioned in the Quran, which also describes punishments for Muslims who commit them.

The last three categories of actions often cause disagreement among Muslims. This is because some actions are seen as more or less severe by different people. Some scholars argue that a particular action is not covered in the Quran. Others, however, believe that, while this action might not be completely clear, it is disapproved of. These differences create differing views regarding many of the issues in society, too.

Inside Islam © Milliken Publishing Company

Words to remember:

Sharia
sunna
mufti
ayatollah
tawba

Sin and God's Forgiveness

Islamic law, or Sharia, also provides a detailed set of guidelines Muslims can follow to obey God's commands. Nearly every virtue is included, and some of those Muslims must strive for are charity, honesty, self-control, and integrity. Dishonesty, violent behavior, selfishness, jealousy, and cruelty are considered sins and are strictly to be avoided.

Below is a list of good Islamic deeds and a list of major Islamic sins.

Good Deeds
Being truthful
Feeding the poor
Returning borrowed items
Studying and learning
Showing kindness to family
Showing kindness to animals
Respecting parents
Giving to others in need

Major Sins
Lying about others
Gossiping
Adultery
Worshipping idols
Disobeying parents
Killing others or committing suicide
Enslaving others
Stealing from orphans

Once a sin has been committed, a Muslim will be held responsible for it on Judgment Day. The only way to erase the sin is to follow a four-step process of repentance called "making tawba." The four steps involve a Muslim doing these things:

1. feeling remorseful about the sin;
2. repenting of the sin by asking God's forgiveness;
3. making amends for the sin, if applicable; and
4. promising sincerely to never commit the sin again.

Sin is considered private in Islam and is kept between the sinner and God. There is no act of confessing to a leader or cleric, as is the practice in some other faiths. The only time a sin might be exposed to the public is when it involves breaking a civil law.

Punishment for breaking civil laws varies. For some sins in which the safety or rights of others are compromised, there are prescribed penalties. These are enforced to deter others from committing the same crimes. Though not all crimes are punished physically, according to Islamic law, repeated theft can result in the loss of a hand.

Section Review:

1. Why do you think the Quran does not address many issues facing society today?
2. Why do you think the last 3 categories of action often cause disagreement among Muslims?
3. How do Islamic virtues and sins differ from those in your religious beliefs?

Essay Ideas:

1. Using your own religious beliefs, discuss some examples of behaviors for each category of actions under Islamic law. For example, perhaps your religion says that God commands you to obey your parents.
2. Write about virtues you believe should be a part of everyone's life.
3. What teachings, guidelines, or beliefs guide your behavior?
4. Under Islamic law, capital punishment is often enforced for murder. Do you agree or disagree with this punishment?
5. Write why you think a dual legal system is or is not necessary.

CHAPTER FIVE

Women in Islam

Muslim women are often perceived as being repressed, having few rights or civil liberties. They are frequently stereotyped as second-class citizens who are forced to stay at home—out of the work force and away from schools and universities. For the most part, these views are simply misconceptions. While it is true that some Muslim women (and men, for that matter) in some Islamic nations are treated inhumanely, the majority of Muslim women enjoy much the same freedoms and civil liberties as Western women.

Men and Women Are Equal— Or Are They?

According to the Quran, men and women are equal in God's eyes. Men must respect women and protect them. Men must also behave properly around women. Men and women must fulfill their religious and societal obligations and responsibilities. However, because men and women are seen as equal, but not identical, their responsibilities differ somewhat. These differences exist because of the physiological and psychological make-up of men and women. For example, it is always important for a wife to have children. She must also control the affairs of the home.

Also, contrary to many beliefs held today by non-Muslims, the Quran has always given women many of the same rights that women in America and other nations enjoy. Some of these rights are: the right of inheritance and ownership; the right to accept or reject a wedding proposal; the right to divorce; the right to keep her own name when married; the right to vote; the right to participate in public affairs; the right to an education; and the right to have a career.

Muslim women also have the right to their own personal identity. This means that a woman's spiritual and moral gains, her successes and her failures depend solely on her attitude, beliefs, and actions. Muslim women today, especially in many Western countries, experience success in such rewarding roles as mother, doctor, accountant, teacher, and politician.

While the Quran states that men and women are equal, it is interesting to note that inequalities do exist between the sexes. The Sharia, or Islamic law, gives men superiority over women in certain instances. Consider these examples:

A man can marry a woman of a different religion, and she does not have to become Muslim. A Muslim woman, however, must marry a Muslim man. Concerning inheritance, men are entitled to a larger share. Muslim men may have up to four wives at one time. Muslim women, however, would be severely punished if they even thought about taking

While Islam does not require it, many Muslim women willingly wear a *hijab* or head scarf to express modesty and religious devotion. Societies that have forced women to wear a *burqa* or face-shielding veil have done so against the true spirit of Islam.

Inside Islam © Milliken Publishing Company

Words to remember:

Sharia
hijab
sunna
burqa
chador

a second husband. A man's testimony in court is twice as important as a woman's. It is more difficult for a woman to divorce her husband than it is for a man to divorce his wife.

In addition to the above mentioned inequalities, it is also said that wives must be obedient to their husbands. Husbands often control their wives' comings and goings, and visits to and from other people, and they can also seek out corporal punishment against their wives if they are so inclined.

On the other hand, Muslim women do benefit from some rights denied to men. These include protection against all men and the right to receive equal financial support when a man marries other women.

Muslim Women and What They Wear

When a Muslim woman walks down the street in traditional Islamic dress, many people in America may view her clothing as dull or drab. Many Muslim women choose to wear their loosely fitting garments so that men will notice their minds and characters instead of their physical bodies.

The Quran requires Muslim men and women to dress in a modest fashion. For some women, this means covering everything but their face, hands, and feet. Muhammad himself once said that once a girl reaches puberty, nothing should be seen but her face and hands.

Muslim women may wear any type of clothing as long as it is not too revealing, tight, short, or transparent. More traditional Muslim women wear a long, loose-fitting type of cloak with pants or a skirt underneath. On their heads they may wear a hijab—a scarf that covers their hair. The hijab indicates modesty in dress and behavior. The wearing of the hijab was the sunna (example) of Muhammad's wives. Though millions of Muslim women don't wear the hijab because it is too hot and bulky, most do wear it, in some form, as part of their religious discipline.

Some Muslim women in Islamic societies can be seen wearing burqas, or chadors. These are veils that women wear to cover their faces. Islam does NOT require women to wear these, and men who force women to do so go against the true spirit of Islam.

The great diversity among Muslim women and their manner of dress can be attributed to several factors. These include the country in which a woman lives, the sect or branch of Islam that she follows (i.e., Sunni, Shiite, Sufi), her personal interpretation of the Quran, and the customs and values of the society in which she lives.

Section Review:

1. Name rights the Quran gives Muslim women that women in the United States also enjoy.
2. What is the significance of a Muslim woman having her own personal identity?
3. In what ways do Muslim men have superiority over Muslim women?
4. What rights do Muslim women enjoy that Muslim men do not?
5. Why do many Muslim women wear loose-fitting clothing and hijabs?

Essay Ideas:

1. Do you believe a wife should obey her husband?
2. If you were a Muslim woman, would you wear a hijab?
3. Write about some stereotypes involving Muslim women today.
4. Many people believe Muslim women are repressed. Do you agree?

Inside Islam © Milliken Publishing Company

CHAPTER SIX
Islamic Sects

Sunnis and Shiites

After Muhammad died, a political (rather than religious) division occurred in Islam caused by differences of opinion regarding leadership. Muhammad had named no one to succeed him and had not established a method for choosing a new leader of the Islamic state. The majority of Muslims, called *Sunnites*, (meaning "traditionalists" from the Arab word *sunnah*, "tradition") united behind one of Muhammad's principle disciples—Abu Bakr. A smaller group, called *Shiites* (meaning literally "party of Ali") believed that Muhammad had wanted his cousin and son-in-law Ali (the husband of his daughter, Fatima) as leader, and that Abu Bakr and the two leaders who followed him had wrongly seized power from Ali. The Shiites believe that only members of Muhammad's family and their descendants are his legitimate successors. (Shiites, therefore, do not acknowledge the first three Rightly Guided Caliphs.) Ali was the fourth caliph. He was succeeded by his eldest son, Hasan, who was succeeded by Ali's second son, Husayn. The assassination of Husayn in 680 marked the decisive split between the Sunnis and the Shiites.

Most Shiite Muslims belong to a group called the Imami. An imam is a religious leader who is without sin and has a direct lineage to Ali. Imamites believe that there have been 12 imams. The first was Ali and the last was Muhammad a-Muntazar. Supposedly, this last imam was born in about 868 and is still alive. It is believed that he disappeared from human view but will return to restore equality on earth. He is still regarded as the only true source of leadership for Muslims.

Shiite clerics help rule the Shiite

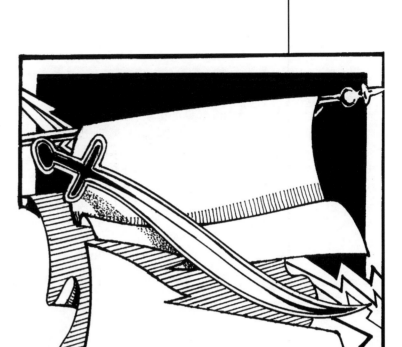

Muslims. They believe their authority comes from being representatives of the 12th imam. Shiite Muslims regard the clerics as having complete knowledge of the Quran and its application. They profit from a religious tax called khums. There is no formal hierarchy.

Sunni Muslims comprise about 90 percent of all Muslims and Shiites constitute about 10 percent. Shiites are clustered in and around Iran and Iraq, and Sunnis are found in the Middle East, Turkey, Africa, Pakistan, Bangladesh, Malaysia, and Indonesia.

While there has been considerable hostility throughout Islamic history between these two groups, Sunnis and

Inside Islam © Milliken Publishing Company

Shiites differ little in their basic beliefs about God, prophecy, revelation, and the Last Judgment. Although the name Sunni suggests a faith more deeply tied to tradition, both sects recognize the same primary sources of guidance: the Quran and the sunna (the example) of Muhammad.

Sufism

A third Islamic sect—Sufism—traces its roots to the Umayyad period of the late 7th century when a small number of Muslims were alarmed by the growing worldliness and luxury of Islamic society. As discussed in chapter 2, the Umayyad caliphs lived more like kings than religious leaders. They built opulent mosques and were greedy for land, expanding the Islamic empire from Afghanistan in the east all the way to Spain in the west.

A small band of mystics protested the material excesses of the caliphs with their fancy silk and satin clothing by wearing woolen robes and advocating a return to simplicity. By the time of Abassid rule in the 8th century, this formerly rather loose movement was given the name *Sufi* after the Arabic word *suf* meaning "wool."

Sufis were at odds with traditional Muslims in a variety of ways. They were concerned that the Sharia or system of laws which governed the lives of all Muslims was reducing Islam to a set of external rules and practices. Sufis bemoaned what they perceived as a neglect of spiritual concerns and were interested in cultivating whatever inner state had allowed Muhammad to receive revelations from God. Sufis were more interested in the Quran than the Sharia and embraced the Quran's openness to other religions and beliefs. Some Sufis, for example, worshiped Jesus whom they revered for his gospel of love.

While the contemplation of God is important to all Muslims, the distractions of everyday life take time away from religious devotion. Sufis strive to minimize or eliminate worldly distractions and believe that cultivating a personal relationship with God is life's highest priority. Sufis achieve a closeness to God in a variety of ways some of which are similar to the contemplative disciplines of Buddhist and Christian monasticism: including strict asceticism (withdrawal from worldly pleasures) and meditation (which can include rhythmic breathing, fasting, and chanting the name of God). The professed goal of these disciplines is the whittling away of the ego or the "dying" of the self such that all that is left in one is God. It is believed that sometimes these practices induce a wild, ecstatic, almost drunken state which resulted in the term "drunken Sufis."

A Sufi known as al-Hallaj (his name means "wool carder") was executed in the 10th century for claiming that the true *hajj* was an inward journey, which did not require the literal trek or hajj to Mecca. The death of al-Hallaj makes clear the history of hostility toward Sufis for their unconventional views.

Despite sometimes violent opposition, Sufism became a mass movement which helped spread Islam throughout southeast Asia and west Africa. After the 10th century, Sufism began gaining momentum—gathering followers and organizing—and between the 12th and 14th centuries, many Sufi orders were founded. Today, Sufism flourishes in every Muslim society in the world and in the West is the object of increasing interest and acceptance.

Words to remember:

**Sunni
Shiite
Ali
Imami**

Muhammad al-Muntazar

**Sufis
mystics
asceticism**

Essay Ideas:

1. Compare the three sects of Islam discussed in this chapter.
2. The execution of al-Hallaj in the 10th century suggests that traditional Muslims may have felt threatened by Sufism. Why might Sufi mystics be threatening?

Chapter Seven
Arab Contributions

As Islam spread onto the three continents of Asia, Africa, and Europe, it influenced such ancient civilizations as Greece and Egypt. These people, in turn, influenced the Muslim world. The common language of Arabic helped unite scholars from all of these countries and allowed for knowledge to be shared.

As new ideas were exchanged, many advancements were made in a number of fields of study, including literature, art, architecture, mathematics, science, astronomy, and medicine.

I. Islamic Architecture

Many public buildings in the Islamic world are given special consideration when being designed and constructed. Islamic architecture has a variety of interesting features and styles that vary from country to country. Important examples of Islamic architecture include mosques, madrasahs (religious colleges), tombs, and palaces.

Mosques are typically the most important buildings in a Muslim city. All mosques have certain specific features that set them apart from other buildings. The courtyard, mihrab, gate, minaret, and minbar are all essential features when creating a sacred place in which Muslims can pray and worship.

Though all mosques are built with certain features, there is still variety among mosques from country to country. For example, some mosques possess large domes, while others sport a high,

Architecture is perhaps the most important and certainly the most prominent form of Islamic art.

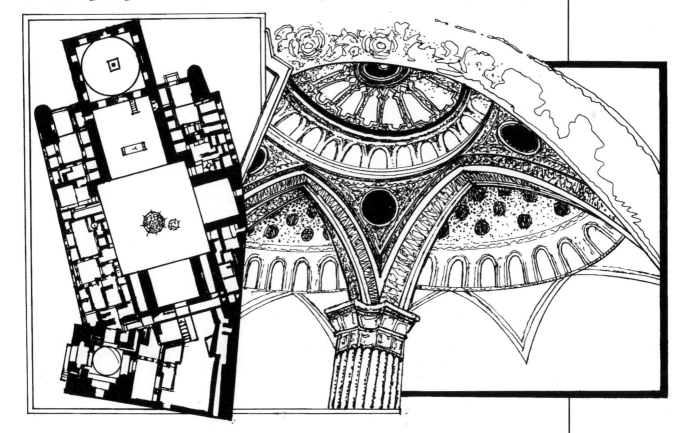

Inside Islam © Milliken Publishing Company

arched entrance with a minaret on each side. Some are covered with ornate tile work.

Madrasahs, or religious colleges, are another fine example of architecture in the Islamic world. This type of building usually consists of four sides that surround an open courtyard. In the center of each side is a large, arched hall, called an iwan. These halls open to the courtyard and are used for lectures. Students live in the areas surrounding the iwans.

Other interesting Islamic structures are Islamic tombs. A tomb is covered with either a square or an eight-sided building on top of which a dome is built. A round tower or one with many sides is also built and usually has a cone- or pyramid-shaped roof. The Taj Mahal in Agra, India, is the most famous Islamic tomb.

Palaces built by rulers of various Islamic countries are also excellent examples of Islamic architecture. Though few remain, one of the best known is the Alhambra at Granada, Spain. It was built from 1248 to 1354. In addition, other examples include inns, or khans, hospitals, and market bazaars, or suqs.

II. Islamic Art

Islam is a very strict religion and its followers have certain restrictions where art is concerned. Muslims are not allowed to depict images of living things. Representations of God, humans, plants, and animals are considered idolatrous and are seen as unlawful imitations of God's true creative power. Islam says that an artist who tries to depict something lifelike is condemned to hellfire. However, Muslims do believe that God is beautiful and loves beauty. These beliefs are reflected in the various art forms produced in the Islamic world. These art forms include calligraphy, design motifs, arabesques, and Persian miniatures and can be found on a variety of products and structures.

Visual Arts

1. Calligraphy

The process of writing the Arabic script in a fancy and artistic manner lends itself to calligraphy. Muslim calligraphers have used the Quran as their primary topic. There are several styles of Arabic calligraphy, and a good calligrapher is highly respected and appreciated.

2. Design Motifs

Because no representations of living things have ever been allowed in Islam, artists had to focus their creative talents on other art forms. These forms include geometric designs called tesselations. This kind of artwork was developed by Muslim mathematicians and involves algebra and trigonometry. It is used abundantly in mosques throughout the Muslim world.

3. Arabesques

An arabesque is a kind of artistic scrollwork that is comprised of winding stems and abstract leaves. The use of arabesques became popular in Islamic art in the 900s and spread to Europe during the Renaissance. Europeans copied these beautiful designs, and this type of Muslim

Calligraphy—"the art of beautiful writing"—and the related art of bookmaking were given extraordinary importance in Islamic culture.

Words to remember:

**Madrasah
iwan
Taj Mahal
Alhambra
Khans
suqs**

influence can be found in cathedrals in France, Italy, and Germany.

4. Persian Miniatures

These small paintings were done by artists who were illustrating famous manuscripts. These artists avoided the realistic portrayal of humans and animals, and instead, made their subjects more abstract and symbolic. The paintings featured a variety of subjects ranging from honored rulers to the average Muslim person.

Decorative Arts

Islamic art can be found on an extensive variety of objects, including rugs, textiles, ceramics, glassware, metalwork, carvings, and books.

1. Rugs

Rugs have always played an important role in Islamic life. People traditionally sat or slept on rugs, and Muslims use a type of rug called a prayer mat five times every day. Thus, Muslims became very skilled at weaving rugs.

Muslim weavers learned to use small lengths of colored wool or silk threads to make knots to create specific patterns. Some of the finest silk rugs will have 1000 knots in a square inch! Weavers often decorated the rugs with gold and silver. Persia produced the most intricate rugs, and these rugs are still admired and coveted today.

A variety of designs appears on the rugs. Common designs include floral designs, scrolls, arabesques, and occasionally, animal and human figures. Many rugs feature a garden-type atmosphere.

2. Textiles

From the 700s on, loom weaving was a highly developed art form in Islamic nations. Clothing, wall hangings, wall coverings, and tents were all woven and decorated with popular Islamic designs.

3. Ceramics

Islamic potters began developing their own special techniques starting in the 1800s. Many of these techniques are still used today. One such technique involves engraving or painting pottery before colorful glazes are added. Another technique, and one that is difficult, is called luster painting. It consists of painting with a metallic pigment on a white or blue glaze. Similar glazing techniques were also used to create beautiful tiles that featured geometric and abstract designs. These tiles were used by builders to create decorative walls and fountains. They can be found on mosque walls, domes, and minarets.

4. Glassware

Glassmaking flourished in the Muslim world from the 700s to the 1300s. Mosque lamps, cups, glasses, goblets, bottles, vases, and windows were all produced with relief designs of animals

and arabesques. Richly colored glass windows were installed in many mosques and private mansions. These windows often depicted designs of abstract trees and flowers and geometric patterns.

Words to remember:

**Calligraphy
design motifs
tesselations
arabesques**

**Persian
miniatures**

The designs were achieved by filling wooden or stucco frames with bits of colored glass attached with wet plaster.

5. Metalwork

Because Islamic religious authorities disapproved of using precious metals to make metal goods, Islamic artisans became skilled at creating beautiful bronze and brass objects. Common objects included boxes, trays, candlesticks, and water pitchers. Craftsmen would engrave or emboss the metal and sometimes used gold, silver, or copper to create inscriptions or designs.

6. Carvings

Islamic woodworkers carved intricate patterns in wood, which they used for doors, boxes, ceilings, prayer niches, and pulpits. They also worked with ivory to create valuable and beautifully carved chests, round boxes, and hunting horns.

7. Books

The Quran has always been beautifully written and decorated with intricate floral decorations and ornate scrolls. Other books that became popular in the late 1400s were those illustrated by the best-known Persian painter, Kamal ad-Din Bihzad. He rendered small, abstract paintings to accompany some famous manuscripts. It wasn't until the late 1500s that some Islamic painters began painting using a more realistic style.

Besides the artistic contents of Islamic books, the bookbindings are usually works of art in themselves. Bookbindings were made with molded designs on the outside and cutout patterns on the inside. Many had gold imprinted on part of their designs. Islamic

Words to remember:

Luster painting

Kamal ad-Din Bihzad

bookbindings

Arabian Nights—perhaps the most popular work of Arabic literature in the West—includes the adventures of Sinbad the Sailor.

Inside Islam © Milliken Publishing Company

bookbindings are some of the most exquisite bindings ever made.

III. Arabic Literature

Because Islam commands Muslims to read and write, Muslim cities have been filled with many wonderful poets and authors for centuries. Arabic literature includes the classical works of ancient cultures as well as the works of its own people.

With the help of Arab scholars from the 770s to the 1300s, much of the learning of the ancient world was preserved. Arab scholars translated many ancient Greek classical works into Arabic, opening the door to a wealth of knowledge for many Muslims.

Arabic Stories

In addition to the classical translations of other countries, Arabs boast many of their own fascinating works, including stories, poetry, and plays. Probably the most famous work of Arabic literature in the West is *Arabian Nights*, also known as *The Thousand and One Nights*. Written in the 1300s, it is a collection of about 200 stories and includes the adventures of such familiar characters as Sinbad, Aladdin, and Ali Baba. These stories are actually fairy tales, legends, fables, and anecdotes that have been gathered from Arabia, Egypt, Persia, India, and other countries. They have kept people entertained for centuries and provide a kind of representation of the many different cultures that make up the Islamic world. Before gathered and combined into book form, the stories were often performed in public by storytellers.

Another type of story popular in early Arabic literature is the maqamah. A maqamah usually consists of short, humorous narratives about two characters who travel to Middle Eastern cities. These characters observe people's behavior and then play tricks on them.

During the 1900s, short stories and novels comprised much of Arabic literature. Probably the most well-known modern fiction writer is an Egyptian named Naguib Mahfouz. This author became the first Arab to win the Nobel Prize for literature in 1988.

Section Review:

1. What is *Arabian Nights*?
2. How is *Arabian Nights* a kind of representation of the many different cultures that make up the Islamic world?
3. Who is Naguib Mahfouz?

Arabic Poetry

Poetry has always been a powerful literary form in Arabic literature. For centuries, it has been recited and sung. Arabic poetry can be traced as far back as the Arabic tribes, during a time when tribal poets used it to celebrate such

The ancient Greek philosopher Aristotle (above left) was as important a figure in the East as in the West. His works were translated by the caliphs as early as the 8th century.

Words to remember:

**Rumi
Shams
Sufi
mystic
Kahlil Gibran**

Below is an illustration of a story called *The Travellers and the Elephant* from Rumi's great poem *Mathnawi*.

qualities as courage, beauty, perseverance, speed, and endurance.

As Islam spread, so did its poetry. It moved into the cities of the Islamic world and took on new themes, such as hunting (a favorite pastime of the caliphs), religion, the fame and glory of the rulers, and the beauty of the rulers' gardens and palaces.

Probably the best-known Arabic poet is a man named Mowlana Jallaledin Muhammad Rumi, or Rumi, for short. Born September 30, 1207, Rumi was a descendant of a long line of theologians, teachers, scholars, and Islamic jurists. At the age of 36, Rumi, a teacher, met a wandering Sufi mystic named Shams who changed his life. The two became inseparable friends, and Shams convinced Rumi to give up teaching. He guided Rumi on the path to God through insight, music, dance, and poetry. Rumi also became a Sufi. After Shams abandoned Rumi, Rumi became very reclusive. He began expressing the painful loss of his friend in poetry. Eventually, Rumi and Shams reunited for about two years. After their final separation, the intense feelings Rumi experienced helped him become a great mystic poet. The utter distress Rumi felt after losing Shams a second time is expressed in some of his finest poetic works. Rumi finally came to the realization that the "friend" that he so desperately missed and wanted back was actually his own desire to understand his own inner self, whom Shams had mirrored perfectly. Rumi died in 1273,

leaving behind beautiful memories of his life with and without his unforgettable friend. His poem, *Rubaiyat*, is considered to be one of the best ever written.

Below is a sample of Rumi's work.

Imitating others,
I failed to find myself.
I looked inside and discovered
I only knew my name.
When I stepped outside
I found my real Self.

In addition to Rumi and other early Arabic poets, the poets of the 1900s introduced such poetic styles to Arabic poetry as free verse and the prose poem. At this time, Arab poets abandoned traditional forms of poetry and began writing poems in a variety of forms and on a new assortment of topics. Kahlil Gibran, Kahlil Hawi, Ali Ahmad Said (also known as Adonis), and Badr Shakir al-Sayyab are several of the most important Arabic poets of the 1900s.

Though the novel, short story, and theater are increasingly popular in the Arabic world, poetry is still considered the most prestigious literary form.

Section Review:

1. What are some early themes of Islamic poetry?
2. What made Rumi such a great poet?

Arabic Drama

Though several types of dramatic performances existed in the Arab world before the 1800s, few were written down. In the 1800s, however, all of this changed. Arabs began the process of translating plays they saw performed in Europe into Arabic. Tawfiq al-Hakim became one of the first major dramatists in the Arabic world. He wrote many plays—everything from one-act comedies to long tragedies. Drama has continued to prosper in many Arab countries since the 1950s.

IV. Arabic Contributions in Science

Once Muslims were exposed to the ancient writings of the Greeks, many new avenues of thought opened up for them. Muslim scholars and

scientists began invading every field of learning, including astronomy, chemistry, math, and medicine.

Some of the many Arabic contributions in science are listed below:

● Using chemistry and magic, Arab alchemists tried to turn various metals into gold and silver. While unsuccessful, their work did help establish the practice of experimentation and the recording of results.

● The Arab alchemist, Jabir ibn Haiyan, was a pioneer of chemical thinking whose works set the stage for the European discovery of modern chemistry. Jabir is noted for his work in the classification of elements and experimentation with their properties.

● Arab astronomers invented observatories, which they used to plot the positions of the stars. They also accurately described the sun's eclipses, and proved that the moon affects the ocean's tides.

Arab astronomers improved and perfected the astrolabe, an instrument originally used for measuring the altitude of heavenly bodies. Arabs also used it for religious purposes in determining the direction of Mecca for prayer.

Words to remember:

Chemistry
alchemists
observatories
eclipses
tides
astrolabes

Abu Raihan al-Biruni

pharmacy
drugstores

Muhammad al-Razi

Ibn Sina

Ali ibn Rabban at-Tabari

Muhammad al-Khawarizmi

algebra
trigonometry
Arabic numerals
concept of zero

- Arab astronomers used and perfected the astrolabe, a device that helped them determine the direction of Mecca for praying. This instrument was also useful for navigation and mapmaking and led to many discoveries.

- Abu Raihan al-Biruni was the first to correctly determine the circumference of the Earth. He also studied the difference between the speeds of sound and light.

- The first school of pharmacy was established by Arabs, who also opened up the world's first "drugstores."

- Muhammad al-Razi correctly identified the source for smallpox and discovered differences between smallpox and measles. He was also the first to classify substances into organic and inorganic compounds.

- Ibn Sina wrote a textbook on the practice of medicine. It was so comprehensive that it became the main medical guide in European medical schools for over 500 years. He was also the first to comprehend that tuberculosis is contagious. Sina discovered, too, that the speed of light was constant.

- Ali ibn Rabban al-Tabari wrote the first encyclopedia of medicine (seven volumes) that encompassed all known medical knowledge.

- Arab doctors were first to discover that blood circulates to and from the heart.

- Muhammad al-Khawarizmi founded algebra, and Muslim mathematicians taught it to the Europeans. He also laid the foundation for trigonometry. Muslim mathematicians introduced Europeans to Arabic numerals and the concept of zero.

One can only wonder what life might have been like without the many incredible, beautiful, practical, useful, intelligent, and fascinating contributions Arabs and Islam have contributed to the world. Many of these contributions are apparent in everyday life. Others require a bit of study to discover. All are impressive, and demand to be appreciated.

Section Review:

1. Why is *Arabian Nights* important to the world?
2. What is perhaps the most important distinction between Islamic art and the art of non-Islamic cultures?
3. What public buildings are important examples of Islamic architecture?
4. What lead to the ability of Arabs to contribute to the world in so many fields of study?
5. What religious purpose did the astrolabe have for Muslims?

Essay Ideas:

1. Islamic art is very geometrical and abstract in design. Compare this style of art with another style of art.
2. Read the poem written by Rumi on page 31. Write your interpretation of it.
3. Choose one of the contributions to the world made by Arabs. Write how life would be different today without that contribution.
4. Arab astronomers named many of the stars as we know them today. Pretend you are a star. Write about yourself and the world as you see it from the sky.
5. Compare the contributions made by Arabs with the contributions made by another civilization.
6. Write what effect you believe the concept of zero has had on the world.

Inside Islam © Milliken Publishing Company

CHAPTER EIGHT
Islamic Holy Festivals and Holy Days of Observance

Muslims observe many festivals and holy days. These events play a big role in Muslim history, beliefs, and practices. Some of them include Ramadan, Lailat ul-Qadr, Id al-Fitr, Id ul-Adha, Al-Isra Wal Miraj, and Maulid al-Nabi.

Ramadan

Ramadan is the name of a month in the Islamic calendar and the name of a period of religious observation. The holy festival of Ramadan lasts the entire month that shares its name. However, Ramadan does not fall in a fixed season, as the Islamic calendar is lunar.

During Ramadan, Muslims strictly adhere to set religious practices that include fasting, reflection, and purification. Adults are not allowed to eat or drink during the daylight hours of Ramadan. They are encouraged to read the Quran from start to finish during this celebration and to spend as much time as possible worshiping in a mosque. They are also asked to reflect on their shortcomings and thank God for his guidance and continued presence in their lives.

Lailat ul-Qadr

This Islamic observance encompasses the last 10 days of Ramadan. It is a celebration of Muhammad's first divine revelation, which Muslims believe he received one night during the last 10 days of the month. During this time, Muslims may spend most of their time in a mosque.

Id al-Fitr

When Ramadan is over, a big three-day-long feast follows. It is called Id al-Fitr. Banquets are held and gifts are exchanged. It is also the time when Muslims must practice zakat (charitable giving).

Id ul-Adha

This observance occurs several months after Ramadan and celebrates the faithfulness and submission of the prophet Abraham. In observance, Muslims slaughter animals for the benefit of the needy.

Al-Isra Wal Miraj

This celebration takes place on the 27th day of the Islamic month, Rajab. It commemorates Muhammad's "Night Journey" and the institution of prayer five times every day.

Section Review:

1. Why do you think Ramadan requires such intense devotion and obedience for such a lengthy period of time?
2. Compare the religious observances you celebrate with those that Muslims celebrate. Are there any similarities?

Words to remember:

Islamic calendar
lunar
Rajab
"Night Journey"

Essay Ideas:

1. Write which Islamic celebration you would most like to observe and which one you would least like to observe.
2. Research and write about the lunar calendar. How is it similar to the calendar we follow?
3. Write about a day in your life during Ramadan.
4. Write about a day in your life during Id al-Fitr.

Inside Islam © Milliken Publishing Company

Chapter Nine

A comparison of Islam with Other World Religions

Thousands of religions exist throughout the world, but the eight major religions (in the order of their founding) are Judaism, Hinduism, Buddhism, Confucianism, Taoism, Shinto, Christianity, and Islam. Each of these religions was founded—or developed its basic form—between 600 B.C. and A.D. 600.

Each of these religions falls into one of two categories: monotheistic or polytheistic. The three monotheistic religions—Judaism, Christianity, and Islam—share another quality as well—all three are Abrahamic religions—that is, they trace their beginnings to Abraham.

Who was Abraham? Believed to be the world's first monotheist, scholars disagree about when (and even whether) Abraham lived. He appears in the holy scriptures of of all three monotheistic religions and historians believe he lived sometime between 2100 and 1500 B.C. Born in the once great ancient city of Ur (in present-day Iraq), Abraham journeyed toward Canaan (present-day Israel) when he is said to have been told by God to "Go forth from your land and your birthplace and your father's house to the land I will show you. I will make you a great nation and I will bless you and make your name great."

Once settled in Canaan (after a challenging and lengthy journey over many years), Abraham was still without an heir as he and his wife Sarah were childless. At the age of 90, Sarah persuaded her husband to have a child with her servant Hagar. The child was called Ishmael. Soon after, Sarah conceived and bore a child who was named Isaac. With

Judaism, Christianity, and Islam all trace their beginnings to Abraham.

Inside Islam © Milliken Publishing Company

Isaac's birth, Abraham banished Hagar and Ishmael who wandered in the desert until they found a sacred well at the site of present-day Mecca. Jews consider themselves descendants of Abraham through Isaac. Muslims consider themselves descendants of Abraham through Ishmael.

Monotheistic Religions

Islam

The youngest of the three monotheist religions, Islam was founded in the early 600s in Arabia by Muhammad, a descendent of Abraham's son Ishmael. At about age 40, Muhammad discovered that he was being called to be a prophet and preach the message of the one true God. Today, Islam is the world's second largest religion. About 1.3 billion people follow Islam, and Muslims can be found in every country in the world.

Muslims believe in one God, and they believe that Muhammad is the messenger of God. Muslims surrender to the will of Allah (Arabic for God). They see their faith as God's final revelation. It is a faith which they believe meets all the spiritual and religious needs of humanity.

The Quran is the sacred book of Islam. Muslims believe that it is the true Word of God that expresses God's will for all people. In addition to the Quran, Muslims also believe that the prophets can help them worship God and follow his commands.

Muslims perform formal acts of worship called the Five Pillars of Islam. They provide the basis for all aspects of Muslim life and consist of: 1) a declaration of faith; 2) prayer; 3) charitable giving; 4) fasting; and 5) pilgrimage.

The two most important Islamic festivals celebrate the end of the month of fasting (Ramadan) and the pilgrimage to Mecca. They are called the Feast of Fast-Breaking and the Feast of Sacrifice, respectively.

The Quran teaches about Judgment Day—a day when all people will be raised to life from the dead and will appear before God. Each person will be judged and sent to paradise or hellfire, depending on his or her behavior.

Christianity

Christianity was founded by Jesus of Nazareth in Palestine. Christians believe God sent his son, Jesus, to be the world's savior. Christians believe that people can achieve salvation through Jesus. Today, Christianity is the world's largest religion.

Christians believe in the one true God. They also believe that God, the creator and supreme ruler of the universe, came to Earth as a human in the person of Jesus to offer forgiveness and salvation to humankind. Jesus is seen as the savior who brings people to God. Christians

Words to remember:

**Arabia
Muhammad
Allah
Quran
Five Pillars of Islam**

**Feast of
Fast-Breaking**

**Feast of Sacrifice
Judgment Day**

Christianity was founded by Jesus of Nazareth.

also believe in the Trinity—one God in three persons: God the Father, God the Son, and God the Holy Spirit.

The Bible is the holy book of all Christians. It contains the Word of God and the Ten Commandments all Christians must obey. It is made up of the Old Testament (the Jewish Bible) and the New Testament (writings of early Christians).

Two important Christian practices include baptism and Eucharist, or Holy Communion. Baptism celebrates a person's entrance into Christianity. Eucharist represents the Last Supper, the last meal Jesus shared with his apostles. Christians share bread and wine during Eucharist to show their unity with each other and with Jesus.

Some major Christian festivals are Christmas (Jesus' birthday) and Easter (Jesus' resurrection).

Christians believe that there will be a final judgment at which time, people will go to either heaven or hell.

Judaism

Judaism was founded by Abraham about 4,000 years ago. It began in ancient Israel in the Middle East. It was the first major religion to teach the belief that there is one God.

Abraham's grandson Jacob, also called Israel, had twelve sons. They founded the twelve tribes that became the Israelites. Many Israelites settled in Egypt where, eventually, they suffered as slaves for many years. They were led to freedom by Moses during the 1200s B.C.

Jewish people believe that there is one God. God wants people to do good

Words to remember:

Jesus Christ
Trinity
Bible
Ten Commandments
Baptism
Eucharist
Christmas
Easter

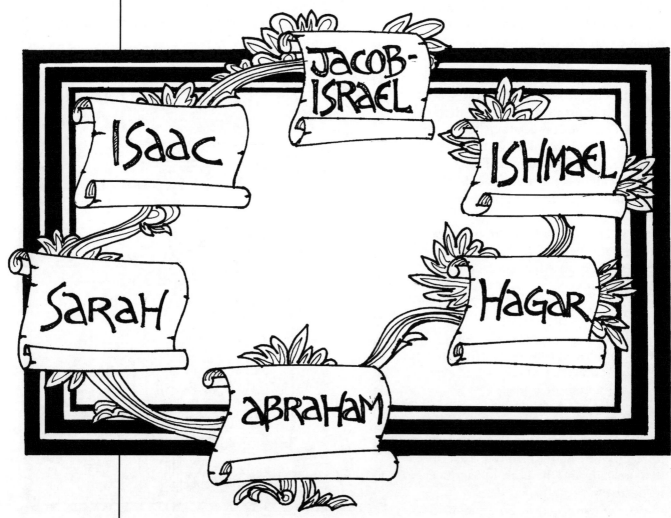

Inside Islam © Milliken Publishing Company

and be merciful. They anticipate with joy a time when God will send his Messiah to announce the final setting up of God's kingdom on earth.

The Torah (meaning "the Law")—the first five books of the Hebrew Bible—is the most important of all Jewish scripture. The Torah contains teachings God has provided about himself, his purposes, and how he wants people to obey him in every aspect of their lives. The reading of the Torah plays an important role in synagogue worship.

Each week, many Jews observe Shabbat (Sabbath). On this day, Jews rest and do not work. They reflect on the completion of creation. The Jewish community gathers in synagogues on Friday evenings and Saturday mornings for Sabbath services.

Rosh Hashanah, Yom Kippur, Passover, and Hanukkah are just a few of some very important Jewish celebrations. Rosh Hashanah is the Jewish New Year. It is a celebration of the creation of the world and God's rule over it. On Yom Kippur, or the Day of Atonement, Jews fast and express their sorrow for bad deeds done over the past year. They express a desire to do good in the coming year. During Passover, the Exodus out of Egypt is celebrated. A feast called a Seder is prepared. Hanukkah, or the Feast of Lights, celebrates the Jewish victory over the Syrians, who wanted them to give up Judaism.

Jewish people do believe in an afterlife, but they focus mainly on this life.

What They Have in Common

Islam, Christianity, and Judaism share a belief in only one God. This type of worship is called monotheism and is in sharp contrast to the polytheistic worship of the other five world religions. Polytheism is the worship of many gods.

The use of sacred texts, or scriptures, is also common among the three monotheistic religions. Both Christians and Jews follow the Bible, though in different forms. Muslims adhere to the teachings of the Quran. All three types of scripture provide a set of guidelines for their followers to use to guide their behavior, with emphasis on ways to worship God and to treat others.

The belief in an afterlife is another shared characteristic of Christianity, Islam, and Judaism. Though Judaism's teachings are not as involved as those of Islam and Christianity, Jews do believe in heaven. However, Jewish people focus more on this life than on afterlife. Christians and Muslims both believe in Judgment Day—a day when all people must stand accountable for their actions. Depending on these actions, a person will either ultimately end up in heaven or hell.

Section Review:

1. What are some important Christian celebrations?
2. What is the Torah?

Words to remember:

Abraham
Israelites
Moses
Torah
Shabbat
Rosh Hashanah
Yom Kippur
Passover
Hanukkah

Essay Ideas:

1. Write your opinion of an afterlife. Does it mirror any of the beliefs in the religions just discussed?
2. Using other resources, choose two of the eight major religions to compare.
3. Research another kind of religion. Compare it to one of the three discussed in this chapter.
4. If you could be the founder of a religion, describe its beliefs or tenets.
5. What religious practices, mentioned in this chapter or others with which you are familiar, do you find most interesting and why?

TEST

NAME: _____

1. *What is the fundamental concept of Islam?* _____

   _____

2. *List the six articles of faith on which Islam is based.*

   _____

   _____

3. *Circle the names of some of Islam's prophets. Put a star next to the first prophet. Underline the last prophet.*

Abraham	Uthman	Nigel	Moses
Muhammad	Michael	Jesus	David
Suleiman	Adam	Thomas	Ali

4. *Write the correct date for each event in Muhammad's life.*

   622   613   570   630   610

   a. _____ led an exodus out of Mecca to Medina
   b. _____ born in Mecca
   c. _____ overtook Mecca
   d. _____ began preaching that Allah is the only God
   e. _____ received first revelation from God

5. *Who were the Rightly Guided Caliphs, and why were they given this title?*

   _____

6. *Why was the Shiite division of Islam established?*

   _____

7. *Choose from the word list below and write the name of the ruling group on the line next to its description. Some descriptions may have more than one answer.*

   a. _____ Islam expanded greatly under these first two groups of leaders.
   b. _____ This group of rulers made Baghdad a major trade center.
   c. _____ They made Constantinople their capital.
   d. _____ This empire completely dissolved after World War I.
   e. _____ Conversions to Islam, at this time, were more a result of personal interaction than conquest.
   f. _____ They constantly fought the Ottomans. Neither side won. Both lost resources.

Ottomans	Umayyads	Abbasids	Rightly Guided Caliphs
Mughal Empire	Mongols	Safavids	Sufis

Inside Islam © Milliken Publishing Company

8. *Write T (true) or F (false) next to each phrase that tells about the Quran.*

   _____ holy book of Muslims
   _____ means "submission"
   _____ considered perfect
   _____ can be changed and added to
   _____ is easily translated

9. *Why do Muslims use a 33-bead rosary?* _____

   _____

10. **(A)** *What values does the Quran teach?*

   _____

   (B) *Name some things Muslims are not allowed to do.*

   _____

11. *What does the Quran teach about Judgment Day?*

   _____

12. *Identify the features of a mosque by placing the correct letter in the space next to the description.*

   a. iwams   1. _____ niche in the wall; determines direction of Mecca
   b. minaret   2. _____ calls people to prayer
   c. muezzin   3. _____ sermon
   d. mihrab   4. _____ pulpit
   e. minbar   5. _____ four halls that surround the courtyard of a mosque
   f. imam   6. _____ tall slender tower
   g. khutba   7. _____ religious leader

13. *List the Five Pillars of Islam and tell what each means.*

   1. _____
   2. _____
   3. _____
   4. _____
   5. _____

14. *What is the Sharia, and with what two things is it interpreted?*

   _____

15. *What is the sunna? Why is it important to Muslims?*

   _____

16. *Write Sunnis, Shiites, or Sufis in the space next to each phrase.*

   a. _____ constitute about 10 percent of the world's Muslims
   b. _____ are mystics
   c. _____ constitute about 90 percent of the world's Muslims
   d. _____ believe in 12 imams

e. _____ emphasize an individual's direct relationship with God
f. _____ developed as a political faction
g. _____ endure tough physical conditions to achieve unity with God

17. *List some rights the Quran gives Muslim women.*

   _____

   _____

18. *The Quran requires that Muslims dress modestly. What was Muhammad's opinion of the way women should dress?*

   _____

   _____

19. *Circle contributions Arabs have made to the world.*

algebra	observatories	concept of zero	chemistry
geometry	lithospheres	concept of fractions	astrolabe
physics	Arabic numerals	biology	philosophy

20. *Who is Naguib Mahfouz?* _____

21. *Write the name of Islam's most famous poet and the name of the most famous Arabic literary work in the West.*

   _____

22. *Why is Arabian Nights an important work for the world?*

   _____

   _____

23. *Circle the types of structures that typify Islamic architecture.*

   | Mosques | temple | shadrach | madrasahs |
   | Hospitals | kami | khans | suqs |

24. *Name and discuss at least two things you think contributed to the decline of Islamic civilization and the rise of the West.*

   _____

   _____

   _____

   _____

Inside Islam © Milliken Publishing Company

ANSWER KEY

Page 4
1. All three believe in one true God. All three originated in the Middle East. All three require moral behavior and devotion to God.

2. The Islamic prophet does not foretell the future. The Islamic prophet emphasizes love for God and teaches followers how to live according to God's laws.

5. Islam threatened the lifestyle and economy of Mecca which was tied to idol worship.

Page 7
1. The Rightly Guided Caliphs had spread Islam to many people and had created an Islamic empire controlled by Arab Muslims.

2. The word *caliph* comes from the Arabic word *khalifah* meaning "successor" or "representative."

Page 8
1. Shiite and Sunni—Shiites believed the position of caliph should be an inherited one, and Sunnis believed the most qualified person should be chosen.

2. There was inequality among Arab Muslims and non-Arab Muslims. This, in conjunction with the development of two branches of Islam—the Sunni and the Shiite—led to dissension among the Muslims. This dissension eventually led to the overthrow of the Umayyads.

Page 9
2. With more people in and out of this major trade center, the exchange of ideas was greater. Muslims were exposed to a variety of schools of thought, artistic achievements, and other advancements they wanted to incorporate into their society.

3. More Arabs became wealthy, and new customs were adopted. This added more diversity to the Muslim world.

Page 11
1. The Mongol empire was so huge and encompassed many different countries and cultures. People from all of these countries began interacting with each other and began teaching and sharing new skills and ideas. All of this led to a diverse Muslim world.

2. Large-scale conversions resulted due to trade and personal interactions.

Inside Islam © Milliken Publishing Company

Page 12
1. The Safavids were Shiites, and the Ottomans were Sunnis.

2. Neither side won. Both sides ended up losing valuable resources.

3. The use of firearms made Prince Babur's army powerful.

4. The Mughal Empire was officially Sunni. However, many Shiites held high positions.

Page 13
1. The Muslims perceived Europe as barbaric and uncivilized, lacking in culture and morals. Napoleon's arrival on Muslim soil was a sign of growing European might.

2. Muslim civilization suffered a terrible blow from the attack of the Mongols in the 13th century. Unlike the West, Islam was reluctant to embrace the Enlightenment which greatly revolutionized and empowered Europe.

Page 15
1. The Quran is Islam's holy book. It is believed to contain the actual words of God. It is the basis for Islamic civilization. It is said to be a series of revelations from God to Muhammad.

2. Muslims believe translations of the Quran are uninspired and unauthoritative.

3. It teaches about God, Judgment Day, prophets, daily prayer, brotherly love, structure of family life, good behavior, organizing society, and applying laws.

4. Muslims are supposed to be kind to all of God's creation, especially their parents and the elderly. They are expected to be compassionate, honest, patient, polite, and courageous. They are forbidden to lie, steal, and murder.

5. The sunna is a collection of the exemplary actions of Muhammad during his life. Together with the Quran, these examples help Muslims lead godly lives, as Muhammad's life can serve as a model by which all people can pattern their lives.

Page 16
1. Mosques are used as places of worship, for religious education, for social work, as tombs, and occasionally as temporary homes for traveling scholars.

2. Some common features of mosques are: minaret, minbar, mihrab, iwams, courtyard, fountain, and prayer mats.

Page 19
1. The Five Pillars of Islam are: (1) the shahada (declaration of faith); (2) salat (daily worship); (3) zakat (charitable giving); (4) sawm (fasting); and (5) hajj (pilgrimage to Mecca).

2. There is no god but Allah, and Muhammad is his messenger.

3. It is the birthplace of Muhammad.

4. Muslims perform hajj to visit the holy sites where Islam originated, to view the Kaaba, and to celebrate God's unity.

Page 21
1. It was revealed to Muhammad more than 1,000 years ago. Our world has experienced so many changes that it would be impossible for the Quran to have addressed the many modern issues society faces today.

2. People interpret things differently. Some Muslims might consider a particular action to be less or more severe than other Muslims. This is how differences are created.

Page 23
1. The right of inheritance and ownership, to accept or reject a marriage proposal, to divorce, to keep her maiden name, to vote, to participate in public affairs, to seek knowledge, to have a career, to have a personal identity.

2. Because Muslim women have their own personal identities, they are responsible for their own spiritual and moral gains, their successes and their failures.

3. The Sharia says that a man can marry a non-Muslim woman, but a Muslim woman is only allowed to marry a Muslim man; a man is entitled to a larger share of inheritance; a Muslim man can have up to four wives, but a Muslim woman is only allowed to have one husband; a man's testimony in court is twice as important as a woman's; it is harder for a wife to divorce her husband than it is for a husband to divorce his wife.

4. The right to protection against all men and the right to receive equal financial support when a man takes more than one wife.

5. So men will notice their minds and characters instead of their physical bodies.

Page 30
1. A collection of about 200 stories that are actually fairy tales, legends, fables, and anecdotes.

2. The stories have been gathered from a variety of Islamic countries, including Arabia, Egypt, Persia, and India.

3. The first Arab to win the Nobel Prize in literature (1988).

Page 32
1. During tribal times, poetry celebrated important qualities like courage,

Inside Islam © Milliken Publishing Company

perseverance, speed, and endurance. Later, hunting, wine, religion, a ruler's fame and glory, and the beauty of a ruler's palace and garden became popular themes.

2. His friendship with Shams and the loss of this friendship; the search for his own inner self.

Page 33

1. It provides insight on the types of fairy tales, legends, fables, and anecdotes that have been handed down for generations by Muslim people in many different Islamic countries.

2. Muslims have limits as to the kinds of images that can and cannot be drawn. Since representations of living things are prohibited, Muslim artists developed a unique style that includes geometric designs, intricate scrollwork, calligraphy, and stylistic and abstract representations of living things.

3. Mosques, madrasahs, tombs, inns (khans), hospitals, market bazaars (suqs).

4. As Islam spread onto the continents of Asia, Africa, and Europe, much knowledge was shared among the peoples of these vast and diverse cultures.

5. It helped them determine the direction of Mecca (for praying).

Page 38

1. Easter, Christmas

2. The Torah is the most important of all Jewish scriptures. It contains teachings God provided about himself, his purposes, and how people are to obey him.

Page 39: Test

1. There is one God, and Muhammad is his messenger and servant.

2. 1) belief in God; 2) belief in God's angels; 3) belief in the previously revealed books of God; 4) belief in all the prophets; 5) belief in the Day of Judgment; 6) belief in God's divine laws

3. Muhammad, David, Adam, Moses, Abraham, Jesus; first—Adam, last—Muhammad

4. a. 622 b. 570 c. 630 d. 613 e. 610

5. These were the first four successors to rule the Muslims after Muhammad died. They were given the title because each one worked hard to help Muhammad achieve his goal of spreading Islam to people in other lands.

6. This group of Muslims was unhappy with and rejected the first three caliphs. They believe leaders of Islam should be only Muhammad's direct descendants. They accept the fourth caliph, Ali, because he was Muhammad's cousin.

7. a. Rightly Guided Caliphs, Umayyads b. Abbasids c. Ottomans d. Ottomans

Inside Islam © Milliken Publishing Company

e. Mongols f. Mughal Empire g. Safavids

8. a. T b. F c. T d. F e. F

9. To help them recite and meditate on the 99 names the Quran gives for God.

10. **(A)** kindness and compassion to all of God's creation, honesty, mercy, courage, patience, politeness;
    (B) lie, steal, murder, mistrust, be impatient, be cruel

11. On this day, all people must stand before God and be accountable for the way they have lived their lives. They will either be rewarded with paradise or punished with a fiery hell.

12. 1. d 2. c 3. g 4. e 5. a 6. b 7. f

13. 1. shahada – declaration of faith; 2. salat – daily worship; 3. zakat – charitable giving; 4. sawm – fasting; 5. hajj – pilgrimage to Mecca

14. The Sharia is the Islamic system of law that is interpreted by the Quran and the sunna.

15. The sunna is a collection of the actions and sayings of Muhammad; it serves as a guide which people can follow to help them live godly lives.

16. a. Shiite; b. Sufi; c. Sunni; d. Shiite; e. Sunni; f. Shiite; g. Sufi

17. Muslim women have the right to inherit and own property, the right to divorce, the right to keep their maiden names after marriage, the right to accept or reject marriage proposals, the right to vote, the right to participate in public affairs, the right to seek an education, and the right to have a career.

18. Muhammad said that after puberty, a girl should cover all but her face and hands.

19. Algebra, Arabic numerals, concept of zero, astrolabes, observatories, chemistry

20. Mahfouz is the first Arab to win the Nobel Prize in literature (1988).

21. Rumi; *Arabian Nights*

22. It is a wonderful representation of the stories, legends, and fairy tales that were popular in a number of Islamic countries, including Persia, Egypt, India, and Arabia.

23. Mosques, madrasahs, hospitals, khans, suqs

24. Answers may vary. Muslim civilization suffered a terrible blow from the attack of the Mongols in the 13th century. Unlike the West, Islam was reluctant to embrace the Enlightenment which greatly revolutionized and empowered Europe.

Inside Islam © Milliken Publishing Company

BIBLIOGRAPHY

Suzanne Haneef, *What Everyone Should Know About Islam and Muslims* (Library of Islam, USA, 1996).

Thomas W. Lippman, *Understanding Islam: An Introduction to the Muslim World* (Penguin Books, New York, New York, 1995).

Myrtle Langley, *Religion* (Dorling Kindersley Eyewitness Books, New York, New York, 1996).

Neil Morris, *World of Beliefs: Islam* (McGraw-Hill Publishing, Columbus, Ohio, 2001).

Seyyed Hossein Nasr, *Muhammad Man of God* (KAZI Publications, Inc., Chicago, Illinois, 1995).

Walter M. Weiss, *Islam: An Illustrated Historical Overview, Barron's Crash Course Series* (Barron's Educational Series, Inc., Hauppage, New York, 2000).

John Renard, *Responses to 101 Questions on Islam* (Paulist Press, New York/Mahwah, New Jersey, 1998).

Yahiya Emerick, *The Complete Idiot's Guide to Understanding Islam* (Alpha Books, Indianapolis, Indiana, 2002).

Karen Armstrong, *Islam: A Short History* (Random House, New York, New York, 2000).

Brandon Toropov and Father Luke Buckles, *The Complete Idiot's Guide to Understanding World Religions* (Alpha Books, Indianapolis, Indiana, 2002).

Translated by Maryam Mafi and Azima Melita Kolin, *Rumi: Whispers of the Beloved* (Thorsons/HarperCollins Publishers, Hammersmith, London, 1999).

INTERNET SITES

Islamic Studies, Islam, Arabic, and Religion - www.arches.uga.edu ; search:islam
Al-Islam - www.al-islam.org
Women in Islam - www.usc.edu/dept/MSA/humanrelations/womeninislam
Islam 101 - www.islam101.com
A Brief Illustrated Guide to Understanding Islam - www.islam-guide.com
Islam For Today - www.IslamForToday.com
Oprah's Islam 101 - www.Oprah.com; search: Islam 101

Inside Islam © Milliken Publishing Company